CARIBBEAN FESTIVALS

A GLOBAL AWARENESS PROGRAM FOR CHILDREN

by Barbara Linse, Dick Judd, and Bernice Gilardi

Illustrated by Jane Caminos, Doris Simone, and Kathy Hester

Fearon Teacher Aids

Acknowledgments

Dr. Don Brenneis, Professor in Chair, Anthropology, University of California, Santa Cruz, California

Dr. Daniel Segal, Associate Professor, Anthropology, Pitzer College, Claremont, California

Dr. Aisha Kahn, Assistant Professor, Africana and Anthropology, State University of New York, Stony Point, New York

Wayne Linse, Teacher of Spanish and English (Grades 3, 4, and 5), West Marin School, Point Reyes Station, California

The editors have made every attempt to verify the source of the folk songs "Anancy and Cow" and "Hosanna" but were unable to do so. We believe them to be in the public domain. If any errors or omissions have occurred, corrections will be made.

Editors: Suzanne Moyers
              Donna Garzinsky

Designer: Michele Episcopo

FEARON TEACHER AIDS
An Imprint of Modern Curriculum
A Division of Simon & Schuster
299 Jefferson Road
P.O. Box 480
Parsippany, NJ 07054–0480

ISBN 1–56417–861–7

1 2 3 4 5 6 7 8 9 MAL 01 00 99 98 97

Table of Contents

* This holiday is usually celebrated in August in Barbados, but because of the limitations of a school-year schedule, we recommend you celebrate it in the spring.

Celebrate Caribbean Festivals!

Most of the islands that dot the Caribbean Sea have had people living on them since prehistoric times. But the biggest population boom came with the arrival of Europeans in the 1500s. They brought with them African slaves they had bought or kidnapped in Ghana, a country in West Africa. Slaves often had to lie in the hold, or bottom part of the ship, for weeks at a time. They lay chained together in nearly complete darkness without enough food or water. Many died on the trip.

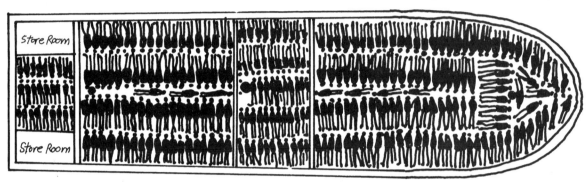

Many members of the Ashanti tribe who were brought to the islands were forced to work the sugar plantations. Men who had once been proud warriors did the work of animals in the field, chopping and hauling the tall stalks of cane. Slave women who had once been queens or princesses in their own tribes worked in the large houses of the plantation owners, cooking, sewing, cleaning, and even nursing their masters' children.

These slaves brought their languages, religious beliefs, food, music, and folklore to their new homes. The Ashanti people were excellent storytellers who used symbols of the sun, moon, creation, and mythical creatures to express their joys and fears. They also used stories to teach their children about nature.

Later, as slavery was outlawed, indentured servants from India were imported to work in the fields. They were paid very little and worked very hard. Their lives weren't much different from those of slaves who had come before.

These groups of people, like people everywhere, created festivals and celebrations to have fun, celebrate special occasions, and express their hopes. Often, holiday customs of different ethnic groups on the islands were blended together into a new tradition.

Today these holidays are not just an important part of island life. They have also become important in the United States as many Caribbean peoples leave their homelands and come to this country. Maybe you even know someone who celebrates some of these traditions. Maybe *you* already celebrate some of them.

About the Format

Caribbean Festivals is organized into three main sections, *Touring the Islands*, *Festivals*, and a *Resource Bank*. Together, these sections provide plentiful background information for you to share with students, plus interesting hands-on activities tied to the food, music, and arts and crafts of the region.

Section 1: Touring the Islands

There are 13 Caribbean islands (or groups of islands) visited in *Caribbean Festivals*, each of them fascinating in its own right. Some of the holidays you'll learn about are celebrated by many of the islands in different forms and even at different times of the year. In general, we focus on one or two specific islands per holiday and how those inhabitants celebrate.

Each of the islands presented in this book in the context of particular holidays are described in greater detail in this section. First, you'll find out more about the ecology of these islands in general. Then you get specific background information about each island's social, political, and historical development.

Possible Instructional Uses

■ As you prepare to celebrate a specific holiday, reproduce background information about the island or islands where that holiday is celebrated. Divide the class into cooperative learning groups. Give each group a copy of the background information and discuss it as a class. Then invite the children to work together in their individual groups to plan an interesting way to present the material.

■ On long strips of mural paper, make a time line listing dates noted in the information. Compare dates of interesting historical events that took place in the Caribbean with similar events in the United States. Let students add symbols of Caribbean culture—including drawings of illustrious people and places—to the time line as they learn new facts.

It's our hope that you and your students will also be inspired to explore some of the other islands, such as Aruba, Bermuda, the Cayman Islands, Cuba, Curaçao, and the Dominican Republic.

Section 2: Festivals

This section contains a yearlong plan of ten festival celebrations loosely organized around the school year (September through June). Some of the festivals will naturally coincide with holiday customs you may be discussing in your classroom and so provide an interesting perspective from another culture.

Possible Instructional Uses

■ Ask students to make a blank yearlong calendar with large boxes for filling in information and drawing illustrations. Each time you explore a specific holiday, ask children to fill in the appropriate month with symbols and details related to the island and the celebration. Display calendars alongside your classroom calendar.

- You may also want to fill your Caribbean calendars in with weather-related information to give children an idea of what the tropical climate is like. Use almanacs and newspapers with international weather listings to add these details.

- After sharing information with the children, ask them to discuss the most interesting, unusual, and exciting aspects of specific holidays.

Enrichment Activities

Hands-on activities invite children to experience the sights, sounds, smells, feelings, and tastes of individual festivals. Children can help you cook up delicious meals based on foods harvested on the islands, plan colorful parades complete with authentic island flags and music, and make crafts in much the same way they've been constructed through centuries of island habitation.

Possible Instructional Uses

- Invite the children to work together on activities in small groups. To facilitate the most efficient use of time and materials, groups might work on activities at staggered intervals.

- Set up a variety of activities in stations around the classroom for children to visit and participate in as desired.

- Integrate *Caribbean Festivals* across the curriculum. For example, following recipes can reinforce math concepts like fractions; learning about rain forests reinforces science concepts; writing letters to Caribbean pen pals motivates students to practice writing skills.

- Work cooperatively with the music, art, and physical education teachers in your school to think of other ways in which this material can be integrated.

Global Awareness

Global awareness questions encourage children to use their skills in critical thinking, values clarification, and comparison. Children will explore ideas about their own culture(s) and those of children living in other regions. As they learn about the customs and traditions of island peoples, they'll also come to realize the diversity of cultures in their own classroom. Ultimately, children will take away a greater appreciation for all of the issues that make human beings as alike as they are different.

Possible Instructional Uses

- Write the questions on an overhead transparency or make a copy of them for each student. Invite the children to discuss the questions in small groups. You may want to assign students opposing viewpoints to debate in teams.

- Encourage the children to write and share their responses to a particular question during a designated global-awareness sharing period.

Section 3: Resource Bank

This section contains complete instructions for many of the activities introduced in Sections 1 and 2. The Resource Bank is organized into the following subsections.

- **Arts and Crafts**
- **Foods, Spices, Herbs and Other Plants, and Recipes**
- **Language Glossaries**
- **Flags**
- **Music and Musical Instruments**
- **Bibliography of Resources for Kids**
- **Bibliography of Resources for Parents and Teachers**

See page 192 for an Index of specific arts and crafts activities, recipes, Caribbean songs, and musical instruments.

Possible Instructional Uses

- Use these resources in conjunction with yearly festivals or whenever you want to reinforce a particular concept or area of study. For instance, as children learn about the flora and fauna of tropical areas, let them try some recipes that incorporate island-grown foods.

- Duplicate and laminate the ideas and use them to set up learning centers in the classroom.

- Send copies of the recipes, arts and crafts, or musical instruments directions home with children as family activity packets.

Create a Festive Caribbean Atmosphere in the Classroom

You'll find plenty of information describing Caribbean ecology in *Touring the Islands* (page 10). At the end of that section are activities that reinforce and enrich that information. Before you test the waters though, cultivate a tropical frame of mind by setting up the following displays.

- Help children paint palm trees onto tall appliance boxes, then set them around your room.

- Or sponge paint mural paper with brown paint to represent bark and wrap it around a tall object like a floor-to-ceiling pipe, a coat stand, or decorative column.

- Ask students to make simple palm fronds or coconuts from green or brown paper, then write the name of an island on each one. Hang leaves and fruits from your palm trees.

- Make papier-mâché coconuts, bananas, pineapples, and other Caribbean fruits (see p. 92) to hang around the room.

- Make your own ocean. Use the directions on page 76 to make crayon-resist murals (or, if you choose, individual paintings) to display in your room. You can also adapt the directions to create a rain-forest effect.

Cooking

Provide a permanent space for storing cooking utensils and ingredients within easy reach of the children. Duplicate, laminate, and store the recipes provided in the Resource Bank that you feel students will be able to prepare on their own. This will enable children to set up the necessary items, prepare the food, and complete cleanup with minimal adult supervision. Make sure a place to display recipes is available near the work area. (See pp. 143–155 for recipes.)

Arts and Crafts

Label and store the arts-and-crafts materials listed in the Resource Bank for children's easy access. Duplicate and laminate directions for the crafts and store them near the materials as well. Children may then make favorite items from specific festivals during independent work times. Display the children's Caribbean creations during your special celebrations or all year long!

Music

Display Caribbean instruments and music books in a specific area of the classroom. Tapes, tape players, and headsets can be set up nearby so that children can listen to recordings that your music teacher may be able to provide. Children can also record their own instrumental compositions with these tools at the ready. (See also the Resource Bank, p. 187, for song book and commercial recording suggestions.)

© 1997 Fearon Teacher Aids

Creative Writing

Supply items such as heavy colored paper, fancy pens, and a word-processing program and computer. Invite students to regularly record observations and experiences as they explore the Caribbean.

- **Journal writing.** Encourage the children to record their impressions of what they feel, envision, smell, taste, and hear during this unit. Children may enjoy including drawings, poems, and stories about the Caribbean.

- **Time line.** On mural paper, make a large class time line to display in the classroom. Invite children to add information and significant dates along the time line as they explore the Caribbean festivals. You may wish to use a contrasting color to highlight significant dates in U.S. history so children can compare the development of both regions. Ask students to add cutout symbols of important people and events in Caribbean history near the appropriate dates on the time line.

- **Letters.** Invite the children to adopt a pen pal from the Caribbean through the organizations listed below. Ask kids to help you collect real objects that symbolize life in America; pack these "artifacts" in a box with explanations and letters from students and send the box to your sister class in the Caribbean.

World Pen Pals
1690 Como Avenue
St. Paul, MN 55108

Worldwide Pen Friends
P.O. Box 39097
Downey, CA 90241

If you have access to a computer hooked up to a modem, telecommunicate with a Caribbean school through E-mail or an on-line service provider. Explore the Internet to find key pal or pen pal connections with students or schools around the world. Start at the Keypal/Penpal Web Resources site: **http://www.pitsco.com:80/keysites.html.**

Other sites to explore include the following.
- *Intercultural E-Mail Classroom Connections* at **www.stolaf.edu/network/iecc** and **www.stolaf.edu/network/iecc/related-lists/PENPAL-L**
- *Kidlink* at **www.kidlink.org/**
- *The Global Schoolnet Foundation* at **www.gsn.org**
- *Project L.I.S.T.E.N.* at **www.lennox.k12.ca.us/listen.html**
- *The E-Mail KeyPal Connection* at **www.comenius.com/keypal/index.html**
- *Kids' Space Connection—Penpal Box* at **www.KS-connection.com/penpal/penpal.html**
- *Netpals* at **www. rmplc.co.uk/meeting/penpals.html**
- *Rigby Heinemann Keypals* at **www.reedbooks.com.au/heinemann/global/keypalt.html#junior**
- *KidsCom* at **www.kidscom.com**
- *Key Pals* at **www2.waikato.ac.NZ:81/education/WeNET/key/khome.html**

Section 1

Touring
the Islands

An Island Overview: Ecology and Wildlife

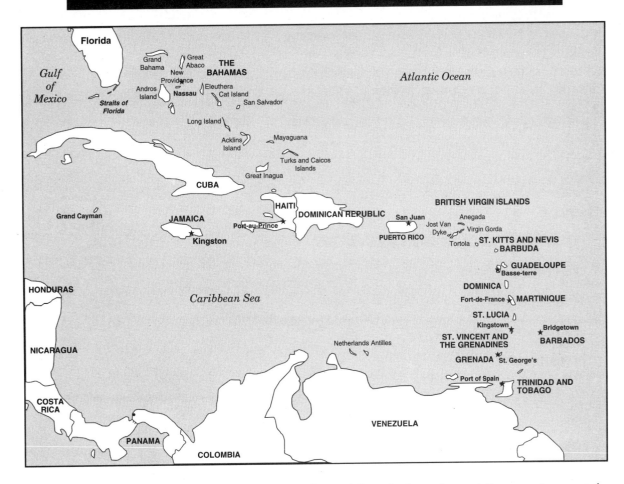

The Caribbean islands lie between North and South America, at the western end of the Atlantic Ocean. At the northern end of this island chain are the Bahamas; at the southern end are the Windward Islands.

All of the islands are really the tips of ocean mountains, some of which were formed by ancient volcanoes. Many of the volcanoes in the Caribbean are still active: Mount Pelée on Martinique; Mount Soufrière on St. Vincent; Kick-'Em-Jenny, a submarine, or underwater, volcano north of Grenada; Hodder's Volcano, a submarine volcano near St. Lucia; and La Soufrière on Guadeloupe. In 1902, Mount Pelée erupted, killing all 30,000 people in the city of St. Pierre—except two. One of these was a prisoner in the town jail, who survived only because he was protected by the thick walls of the jail.

On the volcanic islands the soil is especially fertile because of nitrogen-rich ash deposits. Plenty of rainfall and freshwater rivers also help make these islands good places to grow crops. Other islands developed over coral banks or reefs that formed over thousands of years. These coral islands are drier and not as fertile as their volcanic neighbors.

The Caribbean lies near the Tropic of Cancer, a place near the equator that receives direct sunlight year-round. The average temperature on most of the islands is about 77°F (25°C).

Plant and Animal Life

There are rain forests on many Caribbean islands, including Puerto Rico, Guadeloupe, and Martinique. These tropical forests are so overgrown with plants that water never fully evaporates; the humidity of these islands makes it seem like it's always raining! The Caribbean forests are full of birds, animals, and plants, such as ferns, lichens, bromeliads (pineapples, Spanish moss, and orchids) and breadfruit, mango, guava, papaya, passion fruit, and banana trees.

Though Caribbeans keep pets like dogs, cats, and goats in and around their homes, there aren't any large mammals native to the islands. But there are many other living things that thrive in the lush climate. Some of these include the following.

Birds

- black-headed gulls
- flamingos
- frigates
- hummingbirds
- parrots
- scarlet ibises

hummingbird

parrot

Fish

- angelfish
- butterfly fish
- great barracuda
- parrotfish
- pilotfish
- shark
- snapper
- Spanish hogfish
- triggerfish

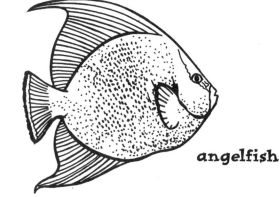

angelfish

pilotfish

Other Sea Creatures

- conch
- dolphin
- ghost crab
- green turtle
- Portuguese man-of-war
- shrimp
- spiny lobster
- squid

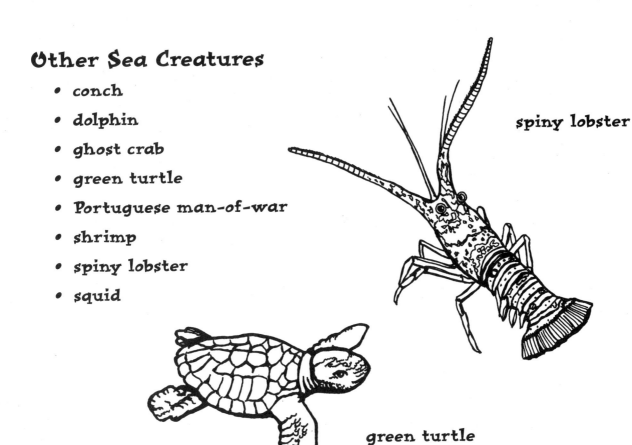

spiny lobster

green turtle

Coral

Coral starts off as many little marine animals called polyps that use the lime in ocean waters to build skeletons around themselves. These animals can live for long periods of time, so many coral skeletons become extremely thick before they stop growing.

Not all coral builds its own skeleton. If you snorkel underwater in the Caribbean, you'll also see purple, red, and blue sea fans and feathers waving in the current.

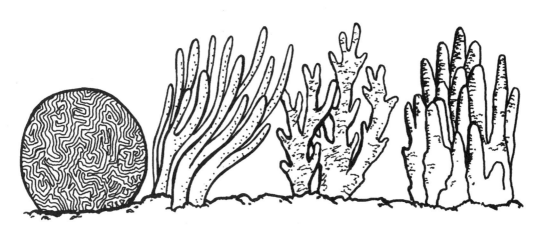

brain coral   **sea whips**   **fire coral**   **cathedral coral**

Bahamas

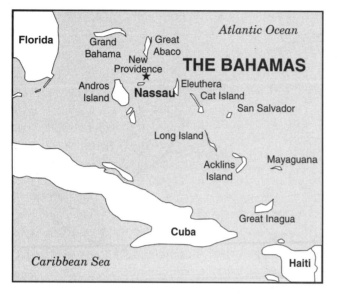

About 700 islands and 2,000 cays (or "keys" as they are sometimes called) make up the Caribbean region known as the Bahamas. The islands lie southeast of Florida and north of Cuba. The Turks and Caicos Islands are still British colonies, but the other islands are independent.

Columbus discovered the Bahamas in 1492, when he landed on San Salvador. The Spanish visited the islands mostly to capture Arawak natives to sell as slaves in other countries and colonies.

There were a few settlers on the Bahamas in those early years, and they had to deal with the wild pirates who relaxed there between raids of other islands. Even after King Charles II gave the Bahamas to the governors of North and South Carolina, people had a hard time settling there because of the pirates. One of the most famous pirates of the Bahamas was Edward Teach, also known as Blackbeard. Eventually the pirates either left the islands or settled down to become respectable citizens. Today almost all the people who live on the Bahamas are of African descent or a mixture of African and European cultures. The official language is English.

The islands became famous again in the 1920s for supplying rum during Prohibition, when drinking alcohol was against the law and liquor was hard to get. The smugglers who traded this dark, sweet liquor were called rumrunners.

The islands of the Bahamas are rich in mangrove swamps, fine white beaches, and coral reefs. One of the hundreds of little islands that make up the Bahamas is called Ocean Cay. Even though no one lives there, this island is very important to Bahamians because it is where sand is harvested. Sand from the Bahamas is exported all over the world, where it is used for making bricks, cement, and other construction materials. The Bahamas is also one of the world's greatest salt producers. Sea water flows into shallow ponds, which are then blocked off so the water can evaporate, leaving salt behind.

Barbados

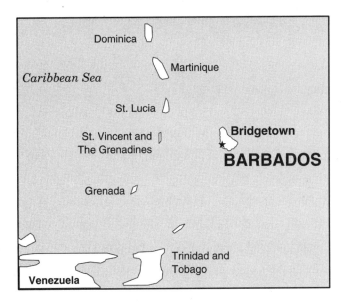

Dominica

Martinique

Caribbean Sea

St. Lucia

St. Vincent and
The Grenadines

Bridgetown

★

BARBADOS

Grenada

Trinidad and
Tobago

Venezuela

Barbados is considered by some to be the Caribbean's loveliest jewel. The people who live in Barbados, called *Barbadians*, or *Bajans*, are just as interesting. Many of them are descended from African slaves, as well as people from other ethnic groups who have visited the islands over the centuries—including Dutch, French, and Asian settlers.

The island of Barbados was formed by the buildup of coral on a base of ancient rock. Natives called Arawaks lived on this island long before Europeans came. They didn't leave many clues about their lives because they did not use writing, but it is believed they were peaceful people.

In 1536 a Portuguese explorer named Pedro á Campos landed on the island en route to Brazil. His sailors called the island Los Barbados meaning "the bearded ones," because of the aerial roots of the ficus trees there—they looked like beards! Like other Europeans after him, á Campos captured many of the native people and sent them to work as slaves on the plantations of other islands.

The British settled Barbados around 1624. They planted tobacco, cotton, sugar, and other crops. By the mid-seventeenth century, sugar was the favorite crop because it grew very well in the climate and soil of this island. After slavery was outlawed, machines were invented to process the sugar cane. Today there are six huge sugar mills on the island.

Barbados

The Basic Steps of the Sugar-Cane Refining Process

1. The hard stalks, sometimes measuring up to 24 feet (8 m) tall, are cut down with machines or very sharp long knives called machetes.

2. The sugar-cane stalks are fed into a milling machine.

3. During the milling process, the cane is chopped and ground until it is reduced to a liquid.

4. Sugar cane byproducts are set aside to be used for making molasses and brown sugar later on.

5. A natural chemical called milk of lime is added to get rid of impurities.

6. The liquid is evaporated, and sugar crystals form as a result.

One of Barbados's earliest tourists was George Washington, who visited in 1751. During this visit, Washington caught smallpox, a terrible disease that at one time killed many people. Though Washington survived his illness, "the pox" left terrible scars on his face.

Barbados is the only major Caribbean island to have been colonized or ruled by just one European country—Great Britain. After centuries of British rule, though, Barbados became an independent country in 1961. English and Bajan, a Barbadian English dialect, are spoken here.

© 1997 Fearon Teacher Aids

British Virgin Islands

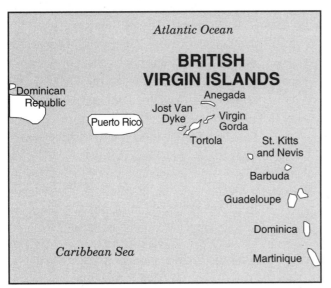

Atlantic Ocean

BRITISH VIRGIN ISLANDS

Dominican Republic

Puerto Rico

Anegada

Jost Van Dyke

Virgin Gorda

Tortola

St. Kitts and Nevis

Barbuda

Guadeloupe

Dominica

Martinique

Caribbean Sea

The Virgin Islands are divided into two sections, one owned by the United States and one by Great Britain. Christopher Columbus reached these islands in 1493, but they were not settled until 1666, when British planters arrived. English is the official language of the British Virgin Islands, but a variety of Caribbean dialects are also spoken here.

Located 50 miles east of Puerto Rico, the largest of the British Virgin Islands is Tortola, which is Spanish for "turtledove." Other large islands are Virgin Gorda; Anegada or "drowned island"; and Jost Van Dyke. Some of the most popular places to visit on the island of Virgin Gorda are the caves, with huge boulders that form the roofs and that are filled with pools of crystal-clear water. The reef island of Anegada sticks out only a few feet above sea level and is very difficult to approach because of the heavy surf that pounds its beaches. The coral reef found throughout the islands is popular with divers and snorkelers. The island Jost Van Dyke got its name from a Dutch pirate.

One of the smaller islands, Salt Island, harvests salt from evaporation ponds much as it was done two centuries ago. The salt was used to preserve fish before refrigeration was developed.

Sailing is another favorite activity among these islanders, as the trade winds provide a steady breeze and the inlets, coves, and islands create inviting nooks to set anchor in and explore.

Grenada

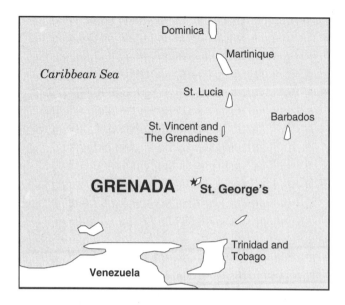

Grenada is known as the Spice Island. Spices grown here include nutmeg (Grenada's biggest export item), mace, cinnamon, ginger, cloves, and allspice. Other major agricultural products include bananas and cocoa. Grenada is also famous for its rain forests, volcanoes, waterfalls, and plantations.

Grenada is a volcanic island located southwest of Barbados, north of Trinidad, and south of St. Vincent and the Grenadines. Grenada also includes the islands of Carriacou and Petit Martinique.

Grenada was visited by Columbus in 1498 and suffered through a tug-of-war between France and Britain for the next two centuries. It was one of the last hide-outs of the Carib and Arawak natives, who by the late 1700s were finally killed, turned into slaves, or forced out of the Caribbean. At one point the Caribs were so determined not to give up their homeland that many of them jumped off some high cliffs on this island rather than surrender to the French. That's how the town of Sauteurs, which means "jumpers," got its name.

Grenada was given by France to Britain in 1783 in the Treaty of Versailles. Its independence was won in 1974. Because of Grenada's long heritage with Britain and France, both English and an African-French patois are spoken today in Grenada.

Many people remember Grenada for the brief war fought here in 1983. U.S. soldiers were sent to the island to set up a democracy after the prime minister was assassinated.

Guadeloupe and Martinique

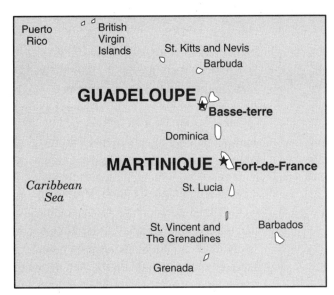

According to Columbus, the islands of Guadeloupe and Martinique were "the most fertile, the best, the most even, and the most beautiful in the world. My eyes will never tire of such greenery." When Columbus visited the island of Martinique in 1502, it was inhabited by the Caribs, who called it Madinina or "island of flowers."

The lush rain forests that grow on the humid southernmost islands of the Caribbean contribute to all the greenery. These islands also contain magnificent mountains formed from ancient volcanoes, some of which are still active. Mount Pelée, on Martinique, last erupted with deadly force in 1902. On Guadeloupe, La Soufrière (which means "sulfur") erupted in the 1970s and still spits, steams, and emits a nasty sulfur stench today.

Martinique and Guadeloupe were both colonized in 1635 by the French and are often referred to as "France in the tropics." The islands elect their own officials to attend the parliament in Paris, France, every year. Many of the homes and other buildings on these islands look like those found in France. In the hills of Martinique stands an exact miniature replica of the famous church in Paris called Sacre Coeur. Napoleon Bonaparte's wife Josephine was from Martinique. She became the empress of France. Today about 90 percent of Martinique's population is of African descent, with the remainder of French and other European, East Indian, and Asian backgrounds. French is the official language on both islands.

Guadeloupe and Martinique are the only Caribbean islands where sugar is processed from a plant called the sugar beet. There is still a sugar mill on Guadeloupe today. Guadeloupe and Martinique also produce more bananas than any of the other Caribbean islands.

Haiti

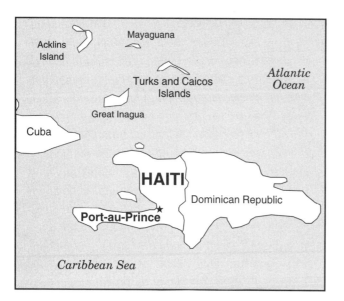

Haiti isn't an island; it is a country on the island of Hispaniola. The word *haiti* means "mountainous land" in the Arawak language. The island's native people were Arawaks, but over the years, Carib raiders from South America and surrounding islands also settled in the region.

Hispaniola was the first island Columbus sailed to on his famous voyage of 1492. As Columbus's men and other Spanish settlers began to colonize Haiti, the once-friendly natives were forced to work in gold mines. During the following 100 years, a million native peoples died from disease and overwork. The Spanish thought Haiti was rich with gold, but after 30 years the mines were empty.

By the 1600s, Hispaniola had become a safe hiding place for buccaneers, or pirates, most of whom were Frenchmen who hated Spain. In 1697, Spain signed a treaty with France, which gave France the western third of Hispaniola. This French colony, Haiti, was then named Saint-Domingue.

The colonizers soon discovered that many crops grew well here because of the fine soil and climate. After about 30 years, Africans were brought in as slaves to work on the tobacco, cotton, coffee, and sugar plantations. Saint-Domingue was producing most of Europe's coffee and sugar.

In 1791, 500,000 slaves rebelled against the French. Other groups joined the fighting, and Spain and Britain sent troops as well. Spain and Britain were eventually driven out, and a former slave, Toussaint L'Ouverture, emerged as the island's leader in 1801. Napoleon continued to fight on, sending General Leclerc and his army. Toussaint's slave armies lost, and Toussaint was exiled to a French prison where he later died. The dreaded Caribbean disease yellow fever then killed General Leclerc and most of his army. Toussaint's followers picked up the fight and finally drove the French army out. On January 1, 1804, Saint-Domingue became the Republic of Haiti. The Haitians were the first slaves in the Caribbean to win freedom and independence.

Haiti is still one of the poorest countries in the world. Several recent hurricanes have further damaged the economy. Still, the Haitian people are outspoken about their freedom and are struggling to establish a democracy.

Jamaica

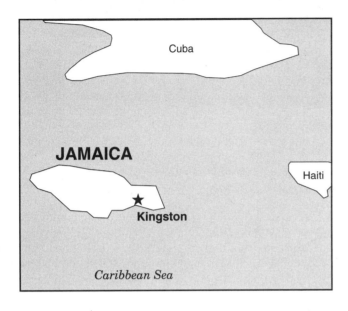

Cuba

JAMAICA

Haiti

★ Kingston

Caribbean Sea

Jamaica was formed millions of years ago as volcanoes pushed the ocean floor above sea level. The Ciboney Indians who came from Florida lived on this island and called it Xaymaca, the "land of wood and water," as it has many beautiful rivers, streams, beaches, and high mountains. Columbus visited the island in 1494 and said it was "the fairest land ever eyes beheld . . . the mountains touch the sky." The Arawak Indians (who came after the Ciboneys) helped Columbus find wood for fixing his ship as well as plenty of fresh water.

In 1510, Spanish settlers brought in slaves from Africa and built a castle, fort, and small village on the island. The island was frequently attacked by Spain's European enemies. Still, the settlers managed to trade with other islands and countries. They exchanged hides and tallow (animal fat for making candles) for cloth, oil, wine, cattle, pigs, oranges, and lemons. Citrus fruits were especially important because without the vitamin C found in certain fruits, people quickly developed a disease called scurvy.

Over the years the French, Dutch, Portuguese, and English tried to force the Spanish out of Jamaica. In 1655 the British succeeded, becoming Jamaica's new rulers.

Jamaica became a haven for buccaneers, or pirates. At first, Britain encouraged the buccaneers, then later it tried to stop them. The center of the pirates' activities, Port Royal, was destroyed in 1692 by a huge earthquake and flooding. A new capital city was created in Kingston.

More slaves were brought in from Africa, including Fante, Ashanti, Coromantee, Ibo, and Yoruba peoples. The Maroons (from *cimarrón*, the Spanish word for "wild"), a group of escaped and freed slaves, fought constantly against the British. A peace treaty signed in 1738 finally gave the Maroons the right to govern themselves and to own the land they lived on.

Between 1834 and 1838, slavery was fully ended. In 1865 a group of former slaves protested their working and living conditions. The British government reacted quickly by punishing the protesters. Four hundred and thirty-nine rioters were put to death; 600 others were severely whipped.

Jamaica

Rastafarianism, a religion with African origins and Christian elements, developed in Jamaica during the twentieth century. Rastafarians wear their hair long and uncombed, in twisted, braidlike strands called dreadlocks. They are also vegetarians and avoid alcoholic beverages.

In 1962, Jamaica became an independent country. Creole and English are spoken here.

Jamaica's coat of arms was designed by Archbishop of Canterbury William Sandcroft in 1661. It has a male and female Arawak standing on either side of a shield bearing a red cross. Five golden pineapples are on the cross. At the top of the shield is a royal helmet and on top of this stands a Jamaican crocodile. The motto at the bottom of the crest reads, "Out of many, one people."

Puerto Rico

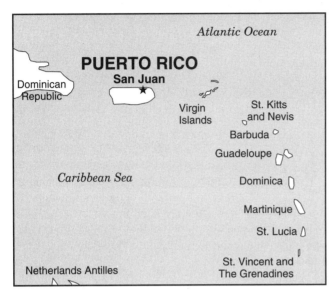

PUERTO RICO

In 1493, Columbus landed on Puerto Rico and immediately claimed it for Spain. He was impressed by the beautiful beaches of this large island.

There were many visits by Spanish colonists during the next few years. Columbus and other visitors reported feeling very comfortable with the friendly Taina and Arawak peoples who lived on the island. According to these reports, the Puerto Rican Indians were among the most sophisticated in the Caribbean. They fished and farmed, growing crops like yucca; yams, a root vegetable like a sweet potato; a local fruit called soursop; and pineapple. The Taina and Arawaks lived on organized farms called *kunukus*. They often barbecued their food—including small birds and bats—over an open-pit fire.

In 1509 the famous explorer Juan Ponce de León visited Puerto Rico with Nicolas de Ovando, the Governor of the Caribbean. Both men were convinced that the island was full of hidden gold; they signed a secret document saying that Ponce de León could mine all the gold he wanted provided that he sent two thirds of it to the king of Spain. But it turned out that there was very little gold on the island.

Ponce de León became Puerto Rico's first governor. From the Indians, he learned how to use the native cassava root to make bread that would last much longer than bread made from ordinary grains. He set up a special bakery to make this bread for the long journeys traders made across the sea to Europe.

Spain built many fortresses on Puerto Rico to keep out intruders. In 1898 the United States won the Spanish-American War, and Puerto Rico became a U.S. colony. Now, Puerto Rico is a territory of the United States. People who live there vote in U.S. elections. Everything that influences the U.S. affects Puerto Rico. While some people want Puerto Rico to become the fifty-first state, others wish it could be completely independent. In spite of American influences, Puerto Rico's core culture is Hispanic.

St. Vincent and the Grenadines

The nation of St. Vincent and the Grenadines consists of 1 large island and 32 small islands that lie between St. Lucia to the north, Grenada to the south, and Barbados to the east. The island of St. Vincent is rugged, mountainous, and thickly forested. It is also home to an active volcano, Mount Soufrière, which last erupted in 1979.

The Ciboney Indians from South America were the first inhabitants to discover St. Vincent (or Hairoun as they called it) and the Grenadines. They came in small watercraft such as dugout canoes, arriving even before the time of the ancient pharaohs' rule in Egypt.

Next came the peaceful Arawaks, who brought with them farming and fishing skills. They may have arrived as early as the seventh or eighth centuries A.D. The warlike Caribs followed, overtaking the Arawaks just before the European explorers arrived.

St. Vincent was known among the early explorers as an island to avoid because of the Caribs. But some explorers still tried to establish settlements there. The Caribs were able to resist European settlement on St. Vincent longer than the people on most other islands in the Caribbean. In fact, African slaves who escaped from Barbados and survivors of shipwrecks joined forces and mixed with the Caribs.

As the cultures mingled and multiplied, a new group, the Black Caribs, emerged. The original Caribs, or the Yellow Caribs, were fearful of them and in 1719 invited France to construct a settlement so they would not be dominated by the Black Caribs. The French brought with them more slaves, scaring the Black Caribs into the densely forested hills for a short while.

The island's troubled history continued with fighting between the Black Caribs, British, and French settlers until 1797. The British forced the surviving Black Caribs to choose between complete annihilation or surrender. They chose to surrender and were shipped off to the islands of Honduras and Belize, where their descendants still live. The few Yellow Caribs that survived this torturous time escaped into the largely inaccessible northern region of the island, where their descendants live today. In 1871, St. Vincent became a part of the British colony, and in 1979 it gained its independence. English is the official language.

The islands are rich in ancient artifacts, or historical objects. Petroglyphs, a type of rock carving, are found on St. Vincent and are thought to have been made by the Ciboneys and the Caribs. On the riverbank near the fishing village of Layou is a stone that stands 20 feet (6.5 m) high and has faces carved on it. The Caribs are believed to have carved the face characters to show reverence for their gods.

Trinidad and Tobago

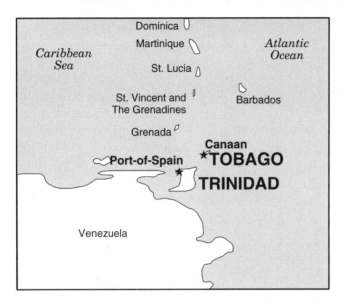

Near the equator, just off the coast of Venezuela, lie the islands of Trinidad and Tobago.

Columbus and his crew thought they could find "the gateway to God and pearls" on the islands of Trinidad and Tobago. When they arrived in 1498, the Spanish found 3,500 Arawaks living on the island. The Arawaks called Trinidad *Iere* for "humming bird." These native peoples lived in thatched huts shaped like bells. Arawak men cleared the fields, hunted, and fished; the women planted, harvested, and prepared meals. Two important crops the Arawaks grew were tobacco and cassava, a plant whose roots could be dried to make flour for bread.

It wasn't until 100 years after Columbus's visit that the Spanish finally established a settlement in Trinidad. They continued to raise tobacco to sell in Europe. In 1699 the Spanish built Catholic missions here and began to convert the native peoples to Christianity. This was an insult to the Arawaks, who for centuries had worshipped their own gods. When the Arawaks realized that the Spanish wanted to rule their land, they began to fear for their way of life. Eventually they attacked and killed many of the Spanish missionaries. Two epidemics later wiped out most of the remaining Spaniards.

New immigrants came from France and England in about 1775, bringing with them both free settlers from other French Caribbean islands and slaves from Africa. When the British outlawed slavery in the 1830s, plantation owners lost their free labor. In 1845 a tall sailing ship landed at the islands, bringing 225 East Indians to work the plantations. Though these workers were not slaves, they were paid very little money and worked in terrible conditions. Today the population of Trinidad and Tobago is almost two-thirds East Indian.

The shared language of people on both Trinidad and Tobago is Creole, a mixture of European and West African words, including some Spanish and French. Trinidad and Tobago became an independent nation in 1962.

Classroom Enrichment Activities

Sand and Sea

Two of the Caribbean's greatest natural resources are its sandy beaches and turquoise seas. Try these activities to reinforce this concept.

- Research some of the oceans around the world, including those that surround North America. Compare these oceans with the Caribbean Sea. Ask children to use watercolors to paint an ocean of their choosing (such as the Atlantic) as well as the Caribbean Sea. Afterward, they can write paragraphs explaining the similarities and differences between the two bodies of water. Display paintings and descriptions together on a bulletin board.

- Protect a small table (and surrounding floor) with newspaper. Encourage students to make creative sand castings using empty milk cartons, beach sand, beach items (shells, driftwood, seaweed), and plaster of Paris. Students could also record their sand-cast creations in drawings or paintings. Ask them to add words describing sand to a chart displayed nearby.

- Explore some of the simple sand and sea activities available in the Resource Bank (see pp. 77–78), including making sand castles, sand candles, and sand paintings.

Build a Volcano!

Explain to children that real lava flows out of the earth's core; in real life, nothing is put into the cone that causes the reaction. Point out that real lava flowing up and out of the cone eventually cools and hardens, building new land over time. (See p. 79 for directions to make a classroom volcano.)

Fish Business

Copy for each student (or groups of students) pictures of the fish on page 12 and pages 85–86 in the Resource Bank. Ask children to use an encyclopedia or other reference resources to find out how to color each fish. Encourage students to find out about other kinds of Caribbean fish and sea life as well. Students can use their research to make fish flags (see p. 87) or fish mobiles (see p. 88) to use in various festivals throughout this book, such as Regatta, Native People's Week, and Crop Over.

Ornithologists

Turn students into genuine bird-lovers. Use the pictures of Caribbean birds on page 12 as a starting point. Encourage children to learn about these and other Caribbean birds in reference resources. Ask them to share some of their fascinating bird facts, then use their newfound knowledge to create bird mobiles or bird flags similar to the fish items described above.

Rain Forest

Rain forests consist of four layers of growth. (See illustration on p. 28.)

■ Trees in the **emergent layer** can grow as tall as 250 feet (76 m). Leaves on many of these trees are covered by a waxy coating to protect them from wind and sun. Colorful birds like parrots live in this layer.

■ In the **canopy layer**, trees may grow from 70 to 100 feet (21–30.5 m) tall. Most animals in the rain forest live within this layer of growth. Monkeys and sloths spend their entire lives in this part of the forest.

■ Little sunlight ever reaches the **understory layer** of the rain forest. Plants and trees seldom reach over 15 feet (4.5 m) in height. Animals like anteaters, boa constrictors, and ocelots live in this layer.

■ Ferns, mosses, and low-lying plants inhabit the **forest floor**. Leaves that fall from the trees above quickly decompose in the 80°F (26.6°C) temperature and 90 percent humidity. The rich soil that forms from the decayed plants is perfect for mushrooms and the tiny seedlings that may one day become giant trees. Animals like rabbits, frogs, and tapirs as well as predators like big cats and poisonous snakes live in abundance in this part of the rain forest.

It is estimated that half of the moisture that falls in the rain forest is created by the forest itself. To demonstrate how this happens, make a miniature rain forest (see p. 75). In this terrarium rain forest, plants absorb water from the soil and send it to their leaves. The leaves give off the water as vapor, and soon water droplets appear on the inside of the jar. Since the water droplets cannot escape from the jar, they fall back to the soil and continue the cycle.

Decorate your classroom to make it look like a rain forest.

■ Hang butcher paper along the walls of the room. (The more walls you cover, the more impressive the rain-forest effect.) You can also hang strips of butcher paper vertically like vines.

■ Ask children to draw rain forest-tree trunks and vines on construction paper. Enlarge the leaf patterns on page 74 in the Resource Bank. Let children trace and cut out leaves from various shades of green paper, then add them to tree trunks.

■ Have children research, draw, and cut out ferns, tropical fruits, and other Caribbean vegetation from construction paper.

■ Add construction-paper Caribbean animals, birds, and reptiles to the rain-forest layers.

■ Hang construction-paper vines and leaves from the room's ceiling.

Rain Forest Layers

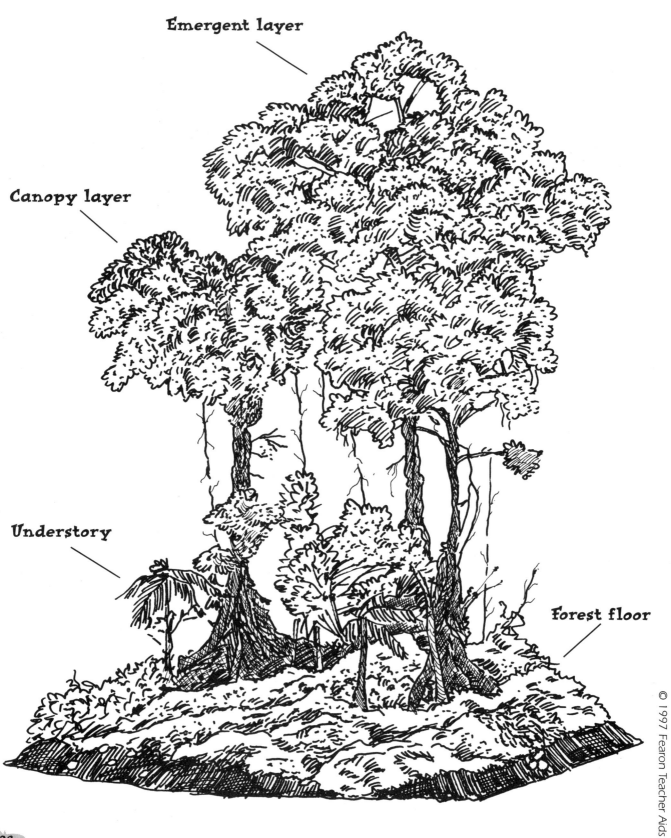

Emergent layer

Canopy layer

Understory

Forest floor

Global Awareness

1. Today most of the Caribbean islands are independent from the European countries that once claimed them, just as America is now independent from countries like England and Holland. Even so, these European cultures still influence people and events on the islands.

- Find out where the Dutch settled in the Caribbean and on North America. Who was Peter Stuyvesant and how is he connected to the Caribbean? Why is December 6 important to children celebrating Christmas in the Dutch tradition?

- Find out where people from Denmark (called Danes or Danish) settled in the Caribbean. Why is the St. John's Rebellion of 1773 an important date in Caribbean history? When and why did the Danish West Indies become the U.S. Virgin Islands?

- Today the French Caribbean islands form two Departments of France. Find out what part the French played in the history and culture of the Caribbean.

2. People from England, Ireland, Scotland, and Wales came as settlers to the Caribbean. Some were sailors or merchants; others were plantation owners, peddlers, artisans, and shopkeepers just like the British colonists of North America. Where did many of the British colonists who were loyal to King George III go to live after the American Revolution? Who was Alexander Hamilton? Where was he born?

3. Spanish culture is still very much alive on Caribbean islands like Cuba and Puerto Rico. Look at a map of the Caribbean and find names that seem to come from the Spanish language. If you don't speak Spanish, use a Spanish-English dictionary to translate the names. Compare what you know about the islands (and their histories) to decide why these word names were chosen for certain places.

4. Jamaica is the birthplace of Rastafarianism. Rastafarians speak a form of Jamaican creole called Capsule Rasta Talk. Explore library or Internet resources to learn more about the Rastafarian religion, language, and customs. Use the Capsule Rasta Talk glossary (see p. 161 in the Resource Bank) and other information learned to write short sketches describing this culture.

5. Research the flags of the Caribbean islands. Find out about their designs, colors, symbols, and histories. (To start, see pp. 177–178.) Compare these flags to those of the United States and European countries, such as Great Britain, France, and Spain. Do any of the flags share common design elements? Why might this be?

Section 2

Festivals

Hosay

Trinidad • Tobago • Jamaica

Hosay is a Shiite Muslim celebration brought to Trinidad and Tobago by the East Indians who originally came to work on the great cocoa and sugar plantations.

Hosay is observed in memory of the death of two grandsons of the Muslim prophet Mohammed—Hussan and Hussein. In fact, the word *hosay* comes from the word *hussan*.

Muslims believe that a drop of blood falls on the earth to remind people of these deaths. Just before the Hosay celebration, people fast, or stop eating for a period of time, to purify their bodies and souls.

At one time, Hosay was a sad observance. Today it is usually a joyful, multiethnic celebration. One of the most important public parts of the festival is the big parade held each night. Before the parade, people eat *melida*, a combination of burnt sugar, flour dough, and molasses. People also burn dried spices called incense to scent the air and drive away evil spirits.

On the first night of the festival, celebrants parade around the streets with colorful flags. During the parade on the second night, people dance with *tadjahs* on their heads. A tadjah is a sculpture made of bamboo, colored tissue paper, tin foil, crepe paper, and mirrors. Touching a tadjah is sort of like giving a toast.

On the third night the people bring forth a huge, magnificent tadjah measuring anywhere from 6 to 15 feet (2–4.5 m) tall. It's a model of the domed tomb of Mohammed's grandson, Hussein. The procession continues as drummers beat on the *tassa*, a drum made of clay, and a *dhol*, a double-headed skin drum from East India. In India the procession on the fourth night ends when the tadjah is dumped into a river or other body of water. This is done because those bodies of water are believed to be holy.

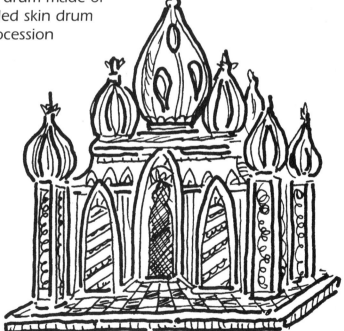

a tadjah

Classroom Enrichment Activities

Make Colorful Island Flowers

The rainy season in the Caribbean is April to September. About the time of the Hosay festival, the islands come alive with color. Add bromeliads and frangipani, two colorful island flowers, to your classroom rain forest (see pp. 82–84 in the Resource Bank).

Do a Dance

Let students pantomime fire-stick dancing (called *ghadka*), in which paraders dance dramatically inside a circle, many of them wearing a tadjah. (To make a tadjah for your dance, see p. 93.)

Papier-mâché Butterflies

Make hordes of molded butterflies for your Hosay festival with thick stacks of papier-mâché (see p. 89 in the Resource Bank). Decorate with markers, tempera paint, glitter, nail polish, and ribbon.

Flag Night Festivities

Flag Night is held on the first night of Hosay. People decorate their homes with "house flags" symbolizing the stories of their ancestors and families.

- Ask students to use family symbols of their own to design personalized flags or family crests. Students could also use symbols of Trinidad and Tobago (fish, rain-forest plants, coral reefs, the scarlet ibis, steel band, calypso) on their flags or coats of arms.

- Use a form of batik, an East Indian art form originally from Java, to make your family flags. Sketch symbols onto flags with white or clear wax crayons and cover with watercolors. Or, after making designs with crayons, dip the flag into a bucket of dye, wring out excess and hang to dry. Your flags will be wrinkled, which adds to the batik look. (See p. 94 in the Resource Bank for complete instructions.)

- Use cardboard tubes or simple dowel sticks to hold flags. Make a wattle (see p. 117) for carrying the flags.

Caribbean Scents

Fill the air with the smells of Trinidad and Tobago.

▪ Place allspice, cloves, cinnamon, curry, and nutmeg in a saucepan of water and bring to a boil. Let your concoction simmer all day.

▪ Or make spice-herb incense bags to ward off evil spirits. Combine 1/3 cup (82.5 ml) ground cloves, 1/3 cup (82.5 ml) lavender, and 1/3 cup (82.5 ml) cinnamon in a tin can. Store for two or more weeks in a dry place. Wrap mixture in cheesecloth and tie with a string for "steeping."

March to a Calypso Beat

The drummer sets the tempo during the final Hosay procession.

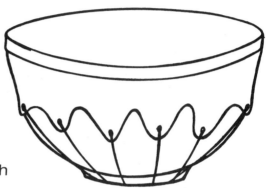

▪ Ask children how they might make their own drums for your festival. Or use the instructions found in the Resource Bank on page 176 to create tassa drums.

▪ See page 169 for a typical calypso beat to try, or if possible, play steel band recordings for students to accompany with their handmade instruments. (See the Bibliography of Resources for Parents and Teachers, on page 187.)

Curry Up!

Curry is a typical East Indian dish, but it has its own distinctive taste when combined with Caribbean fruits and spices. For recipes to try, see pages 143 and 149.

Global Awareness

1. East Indians who settled in Trinidad and Tobago came from the continent of Asia. In the United States there are many Asian immigrants who continue to celebrate their holidays as they did in their homelands.

- When is the Chinese New Year celebrated in the United States?

- How is the Chinese New Year celebration in the United States similar to the Hosay Festival in Trinidad and Tobago? How are they different?

2. The festival of Hosay is a sad remembrance. It honors the memory of Hussan and Hussein, the grandsons of the Muslim prophet Mohammed, who were murdered in 680 A.D. People who are murdered in the name of a cause they believe in are sometimes called martyrs.

- In the United States, Valentine's Day and Saint Patrick's Day were originally celebrated to honor a Christian martyr and saint. Find out when these people lived and what they believed in.

- What special foods, music, and symbols are used to honor St. Valentine and St. Patrick?

3. Today, Pakistan is a separate Muslim country formed when India received its independence from Great Britain, in 1947. Most of the rest of India is Hindu, a different religion from Islam. The Muslim indentured servants from India who came to work in the West Indies after the British outlawed slavery settled mostly in Trinidad and Tobago, Jamaica, and British Guyana (now Belize). Today there are many Muslims living in the United States.

- Besides India and Pakistan, from what other countries did American Muslims emigrate? Why did they immigrate to the United States?

- What holidays do Muslims celebrate?

- What is Ramadan?

© 1997 Fearon Teacher Aids

Pirate Week

British Virgin Islands • Bahamas • Puerto Rico

Privateers, Buccaneers, and Pirates

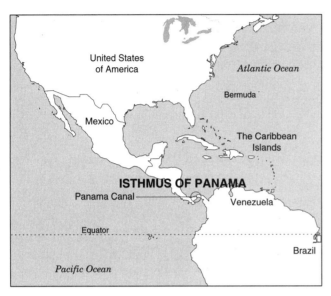

European countries like England and Spain could barely wait to begin trading the riches they discovered on the Caribbean islands. They had already become wealthy from the jewels, silver, gold, and spices they had found on the Pacific Coast and in Central and South America.

But traveling in the 1500s and 1600s was not easy. To get from the Pacific Ocean to the Atlantic Ocean, for instance, a ship had to travel around the tip of South America— unless it used the Isthmus of

Panama. This little strip of land between the Pacific Coast and the Gulf of Mexico was used by traders and explorers as a shortcut between the Atlantic and Pacific Oceans. It was so important that countries often fought over who would own it.

Galleons stopped at the isthmus, and sailors carried the treasures they had

collected to ships that would take them east. These ships, as well as those returning from Central and South America, sailed in and out of ports like Port Royal and Kingston, Jamaica. There the sailors would rest and refresh themselves as they gathered even more trade goods from the Caribbean.

Pirate Week

All of these expensive comings and goings were very tempting to a group of people called sea robbers, or pirates. They would attack ships, kill their crews, and steal everything on-board. If they were caught, pirates were often put to death. Privateers were people hired by the government of one's country to steal cargo from the ships of other countries. Even though they weren't exactly illegal, privateers were still corrupt and often cruel to their victims.

One group of pirates was known as buccaneers. The buccaneers got their name from *boucane*, the French word for "meat," because they often cooked their meat outdoors over an open fire. The buccaneers called their group the Brotherhood of the Sea.

Buccaneers and pirates often hid their treasure, but many were killed or imprisoned before they could return to recover it. Some people believe much of this treasure is still waiting to be found in caves and coves on many of the secluded Caribbean islands.

Women as Pirates

People rarely think of women as pirates. In fact, one of the Shipboard Rules of Pirates (see p. 41) forbids women from coming aboard. However, there were exceptions to this rule. Two pirate women we know about were Anne Bonny and Mary Read. They dressed like men, were excellent shooters, and could fight as well as any man. They were caught and put on trial for piracy, but weren't executed like their fellow pirates because they were both pregnant at the time.

Classroom Enrichment Activities

Celebrate Barbecue

Cooking in the open air was the most practical way for busy privateers to eat. The weather was warm, there were plenty of fish and rabbits to catch, and heavily-salted beef or pork was available from whatever ships the pirates captured. Pirates were also fond of the guavas, mangoes, and pineapples that littered the Caribbean beaches. They would often cook these fruits with the meat and vegetables, inventing the earliest form of tangy Caribbean barbecue sauce. For a barbecue recipe, see page 151.

Dressing the Part

Officers

The traditional pirate's hat had a floppy brim trimmed with an ostrich plume, leaving the pirate's face exposed. Officers also wore sashes crossing their chests, mostly for the purpose of holding several handguns, since each gun had to be reloaded after a single volley of shot. The officers wore knee-length waistcoats decorated with braid and lots of buttons, and breeches with tightfitting hose. Shoes often had large buckles and heels quite a bit higher than those men wear today. Swords were carried in sheaths hung from belts.

Common Pirate

The stereotype of the pirate wearing a black patch over his eye is not far from the truth. Years of constant fighting and poor medical care often resulted in missing eyes and deep, ugly scars. Most pirates covered their heads with a bandanna tied near one ear. They often wore T-shirts and breeches.

Pirate Flags

Most pirates designed their own special flags to fly on their ships. They hoped that these creepy designs would frighten people so much that they would give up their loot without much of a fight.

Stede Bonnot   Thomas Tew   John Rackham   Blackbeard   Henry Every

- Ask children to think of personal qualities they would like people to know about themselves; for instance, that they are artistic, athletic, or friendly. Children can then choose one color of construction paper that they think reflects this trait (for example, a friendly person might choose yellow). On contrasting colors of paper, students can draw bold symbols of the personal traits they want to advertise on their flags. A friendly person might choose symbols depicting a handshake or smile. Have students cut their symbols out and paste them onto the flag backgrounds.

Now ask students to think of a special name that reflects their personal qualities or physical attributes, much as a pirate would. Some examples of real pirate nicknames include Calico Jack and Blackbeard.

Hang up the flags, labeled with student nicknames, on a bulletin board surrounded by real pirate flags.

Treasure Hunt

In small groups, children can put together a treasure box of Caribbean symbols. Ask them to decide where in your school they might hide their treasure chests, then make maps based on the terrain of the classroom or school grounds to help lead classmates to these treasures. (See pp. 119–120 in the Resource Bank.)

- Children could incorporate features of the classroom to make up names for specific locations, such as Math Center Mountain, Crooked Cubby Cove, Messy Desk Marsh, and so on.

- Ask students to write legends for their maps. For instance, to show that the treasure hunter must proceed through a noisy area of the classroom, they might create a symbol that looks like an ear. To show that the map reader will have to look carefully to find a clue, the legend could include a symbol that looks like two eyes.

Music

Sing some sea chanteys. (See "Boston Come All Ye," on p. 166, and the Bibliography of Resources for Parents and Teachers, p. 187, for songbooks to explore, or ask your school's music specialist for suggestions.) Discuss how these songs might reflect the lives of sea raiders in the seventeenth and eighteenth centuries.

Treasure Trunk . . .

Make a treasure chest and authentic-looking treasure to use in a pirate drama as part of a whole-class scavenger hunt or as a great display in your reading corner during this unit. Or use this idea to display children's work throughout the year.

- Use a medium-sized appliance box as a steamer trunk.

- Spongepaint the box, using metallic paints to create an antique surface. Paint on a lock and use paper strips as hinges. To add even more "oldness" to the trunk, dip a stiff toothbrush in dark brown or black paint and fleck it onto the surface.

- After three or four days, carefully cut three sides off the top of the box so it appears that the lid of the trunk will open.

. . . And Treasure Loot

Ask parents to donate old costume jewelry and other objects. Plastic and glass beads make wonderful strings of jewels that are fun to drape over the sides of the opened treasure chest.

- Make bracelets by rolling papier-mâché over medium wire or tagboard; add plastic beads and glitter. (See the Resource Bank, p. 107, for complete instructions.)

- Make beads by cutting triangles of paper from catalogs with shiny, colorful pages. Roll up the triangle from the wide end and glue the ends together, leaving a tiny hole for stringing the necklace or bracelet.

- Use baker's clay to make coins (see recipe on p. 94 in the Resource Bank). Add symbols that would be found on old Spanish, British, and French coins from the time period (A.D. 1500–1700). When dry, gild with metallic tempera paint and shellac so that they shine.

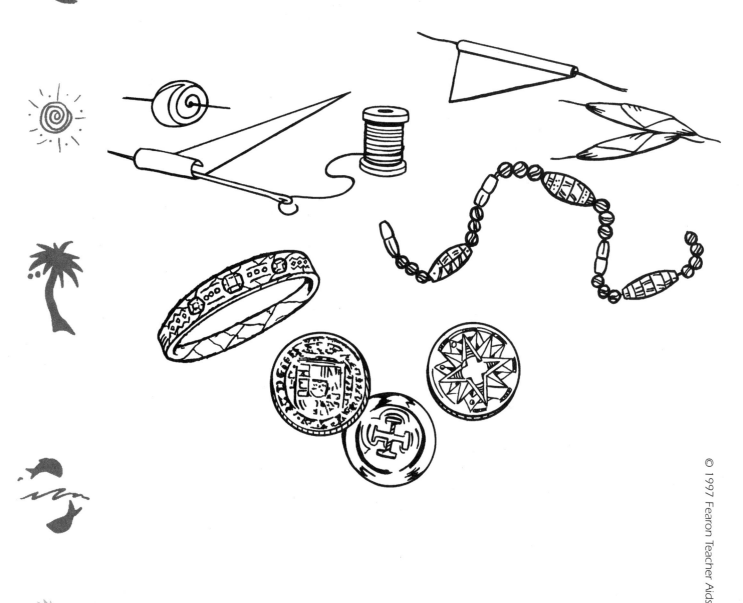

Shipboard Rules of the Pirate World

I. Equal vote shall be had by every person.

II. Each shall have a chance at the distribution of prizes. Any stealing from another will be punishable by severed ears or slit nose. To defraud a mate will result in marooning.

III. No gambling aboard ship.

IV. Each will have weapons ready for use at any time.

V. No women or children aboard except for special socials.

VI. Death will come to any who desert the ship or show cowardice.

VII. Quarrels are to be settled on land, never onboard ship.

VIII. Loss of a limb is rewarded by 800 pieces of eight as recompense.

IX. Captain and Quartermaster each to receive two shares of prizes.

X. Musicians may rest on Sunday unless an engagement is in progress.

Global Awareness

1. Gold stolen from conquered ancient civilizations was impossible for the English, French, and Dutch to resist!

- What are some symbols connected to piracy?

- How could someone like Sir Francis Drake be a hero and a pirate at the same time?

2. Even lawless pirates had certain rules! Look at the Shipboard Rules of the Pirate World (see p. 41). Explain what these rules tell you about the lives of pirates and privateers.

3. Pirates may have been violent, but they often had to be very clever as well. Using your knowledge of the Caribbean, explain some of the things a pirate would need to know to survive.

4. There may not be pirates around today, but there are still treasure hunters and adventurers.

- What do these treasure hunters look for?

- Where do they look?

- What special equipment or tools are needed?

5. Many old shipwrecks are still located deep beneath the sea. Find out what happens to wooden and metal ships in salt water.

- Can old ships be salvaged or brought up out of the sea? What happens to the ships when they are removed from the salt water?

- Who owns these sunken ships currently?

- Can a treasure hunter keep whatever he or she finds on or around a sunken wreck?

Divali

Trinidad and Tobago

Divali (doo WAH lee) is also known as the Hindu festival of lights, usually celebrated in late October or November. The word *divali* comes from the Sanskrit word *dipavali*, which means "row of lights." The festival symbolizes the victory of light over darkness and honors Lakshmi, goddess of good fortune, wealth, light, beauty, and love, who is said to be seeking light during this time of year. People light deya lamps to light Lakshmi's way.

Hindus believe that burning incense all night during Divali will bring them prosperity in the year ahead and keep evil spirits away. Divali is also a time for people to show their appreciation of one another. Visiting the homes of friends and relatives is an important part of this celebration. Merchants are particularly enthusiastic about this holiday, since it is a time for them to celebrate their prosperity.

Well before Divali, people begin scrubbing and scenting their homes in preparation for the arrival of Lakshmi. They paint designs onto floors and walls with rice-flour water. Early on the first day of Divali, the mother of the household sprinkles a little cologne on her children or gives a potpourri sachet to each family member.

During Divali, people may also observe Brother's Day. Women and girls give their brothers perfumed water for their baths, prepare special foods for them, and draw red powder lines on their foreheads.

In 1966, Divali was recognized as both a national holiday and a national festival in Trinidad and Tobago. Public celebrations of the festival are held a few days before the actual date, since Hindus usually do not leave their homes on Divali Day.

The goddess Lakshmi

Classroom Enrichment Activities

Breakfast Bonanza

During Divali, people prepare a breakfast of 14 different foods. Each food symbolizes something important about the holiday. Hindus and other East Indians eat mostly vegetarian dishes supplemented with protein from fish and nuts. During meals, traditional Hindus sit on the floor and use only their right hand to eat; the left hand is used for special cleansing rituals and is considered unclean.

- Help your students plan their own breakfast to celebrate the Hindu culture of the Caribbean. Encourage Indian students in your class to volunteer to bring in traditional recipes. Obtain authentic menus and foods from Indian restaurants. Some interesting Indian foods to try include

roti (a flat round loaf of bread made from wheat flour and milk)

spiced potato curry

chickpeas and curds

rice

- See the recipes on pages 143, 144, 146, and 148 for other Hindu-type foods that the class could prepare for a special classroom celebration.

Good Deeds Journals

Ask children to decide what special jobs they could do for someone this week to celebrate the compassionate aspects of this festival. Have students staple together several sheets of paper to make a Good Deeds Journal in which they record things they have done to help others. At the end of the week, collect the journals and write responses to students, encouraging them to continue thinking of ways to help others.

Make Deya Pots

Light is an important part of the symbolism of Divali. Make the little clay lamps known as deyas using the instructions on pages 116–117. Fill finished pots with either coconut or mustard oil to add scent. Pour melted wax into the pots and, just before it hardens, insert a piece of heavy string as a wick.

Create Coins of Good Fortune

During Divali, Hindus leave gold coins for the goddess Lakshmi.

■ Smear some cardboard or baker's clay (p. 94) coins with turmeric, a golden spice powder from the Caribbean island of Grenada. Ask students to decorate plain white envelopes with pictures symbolizing love, good fortune, and acts of charity. Next, ask students to think about meaningful good wishes. What are the kinds of things people hope will happen to them? Allow students to write fortunes based on their ideas.

■ Collect fortune envelopes and put them in a basket or bag. Invite students to choose a fortune from the basket and read it aloud. After students have picked a fortune, ask them to come up with at least one idea for achieving their good wish in a realistic way. For example, a student might draw a fortune that says "You will become wealthy"; an idea for working toward this goal might be to study hard in school in order to go to college.

■ Conclude the activity by making a chart with good fortunes in one column and, in another column, children's ideas for achieving these wishes.

Puppets of the Gods

Other important Hindu gods are Ganesha, the elephant-headed god, and Hanuman, the monkey god. Ganesha is a popular god and is believed to bring good luck and to remove obstacles that Hindu worshippers face. Hanuman is thought of as a protector because he came to the aid of the god Rama when Rama's army was engaged in a difficult battle.

Ganesha, the elephant-headed god

Hanuman, the monkey god

- Invite students to create paper-bag puppets of Lakshmi, Ganesha, or Hanuman. Use the illustrations on pages 43 and 45 as guides if desired. For Ganesha and Hanuman, see also the outline pictures on page 127 in the Resource Bank. After students have created the basic puppet figures, provide pictures of Indian art for children to look at while they decorate their puppets.

- As a follow-up activity, ask students to find additional information about these gods and goddesses, using resources available in the library or on CD-ROM. Encourage students to write short skits describing the adventures these gods and goddesses might have, then present the skits for classmates, using the puppets they created.

- Make kites featuring the various activities, items, and characters associated with Divali (see p. 123). Students can decorate their kites with pictures that illustrate what they have learned about the islands of Trinidad and Tobago and this festival. Fly the kites to mark the conclusion of your study of Divali.

Caribbean Castles

During Divali, children make model castles out of mud and decorate them with tiny trees, little animals, and toy warriors.

- Ask students how children on Trinidad or Tobago might make their castles reflect the local environment. Study some books about castles and brainstorm various Caribbean adaptations. For instance, the flags that fly from turrets might include pirate symbols or the design of Trinidad and Tobago's flag.

- You can also make a Divali castle in a shoebox. Use tempera paint for a Caribbean background. Make the base structure of your castle from cardboard and cover with papier-mâché. Use pieces of painted sponge for vegetation and pipe cleaners or various forms of modeling clay to make animal and people figures.

- See page 78 in the Resource Bank for directions on building sand castles.

Global Awareness

1. How are Chanukah—a Jewish holiday celebrated by many Americans, Israelis, and others—and Divali similar? Why do you think lamps or candles are important to both holidays?

2. Why do holidays like Divali and Chanukah appeal to children?

3. Around the same time that Divali is celebrated on Trinidad and Tobago, Thanksgiving is celebrated in the United States.

- How are these two holidays alike?
- What Native American foods could be found at both an American Thanksgiving celebration and a Caribbean Divali celebration?

4. Can you think of any similarities between Halloween and Divali? What do these holidays share in common?

5. What other holidays do Hindus celebrate? Are they happy or sad holidays? When do these holidays take place during the year?

6. If you have Hindu children from Trinidad and Tobago in your class or school, invite them to tell tales of Divali. You may wish to prepare questions ahead of time to ask visitors, such as

- Are there occasions during the Divali celebration when family members do special things for other family members?
- What are some of these special things? For whom are they done?
- Is Divali celebrated the same way around the world? How is it the same or different from the holiday you've celebrated?

7. Divali is the most eagerly anticipated holiday for children of East Indian descent in the Caribbean. What is the most eagerly anticipated holiday in your area? Why is it so? Is it a seasonal holiday? Compare and contrast your personal favorite festival with Divali.

8. In Trinidad, Divali is a holiday that is widely observed by people who are not part of the ethnic group that brought the holiday to the island. Hindu families often participate in both private and public observances.

- What ethnic celebrations in the United States have you participated in? How did each celebration reflect the unique culture of its particular ethnic group?
- In what special ways might a family you know celebrate its heritage at one of these festivals?

Jonkanoo

Jamaica • the Bahamas

Jonkanoo is a parade and party usually held in December in Jamaica and the Bahamas. This celebration began during the days of slavery, probably in the seventeenth century. Christmas became the popular time for celebrating the holiday because that was usually the only time when the slaves were allowed to take time off from their work.

It's believed that the interesting rituals and dances performed during this celebration date all the way back to ancient African religious customs. In the early days of this celebration, people would dance around the countryside wearing ankle bracelets made from bells, shells, and other objects that could be strung together to make noise. This noisy dancing may have been done because people believed it would keep evil spirits away.

People who celebrate the holiday call Jonkanoo characters *roots* because they have been handed down through generations from the very beginning of the African family tree. One important Jonkanoo character is referred to as Pitchy Patchy because his costume is sewn from pieces of cloth fitted together like patchwork. Another popular character is John Canoe, a silly figure based on the plantation owners of long ago.

After Britain began to rule Jamaica, British mumming plays were combined with masquerades from various African nations. Also, Scottish kilts, formal dances called minuets, and bagpipes became part of the holiday customs. Variations of this festival are found in many Caribbean nations with a British history, including Belize, St. Kitts-Nevis, Guyana, and Bermuda.

John Canoe, one of the Jonkanoo parade characters, is often seen wearing the plantation house on his head!

Classroom Enrichment Activities

Put History in Its Place

The list of events below appear in the order in which they happened.

Columbus and his men discover Jamaica.

Columbus returns to Jamaica to look for gold.

Caribbean Indians help Columbus find materials to repair his boat.

Columbus leaves Jamaica, never to return.

Pirates come to Jamaica and steal many things.

The English win control of Jamaica.

Many British citizens arrive to colonize the island and raise sugar cane and other crops.

Slaves are brought in from Africa to do the hardest work.

The Jonkanoo holiday is first celebrated.

Jamaican slaves revolt against their owners at Montego Bay.

Immigrants from other countries arrive to work and live on Jamaica.

- Copy each sentence, out of order, onto chart paper. After sharing the information about Jamaica on pages 21–22 and in other reference books, challenge students to help you place each event in proper order. Indicate students' choices by writing a number next to each sentence.

- After revealing the correct order of the events to students, invite students to use each sentence to construct a panel-by-panel "movie" of Jamaica's history (see directions for a box theater on p. 96).

Language

Slave owners believed that by buying their human merchandise from different African tribes, they could prevent them from communicating and eventually rebelling. As the slaves worked and lived together, however, they began to adapt elements of each others' languages. Further blending of languages happened as the slaves learned to communicate with their masters and overseers in French, Spanish, and English. That was how Creole—a mixing of several languages to form a new language—began.

- Before sharing the Creole glossary (p. 160) with your students, ask them to make up new words by combining words with similar meanings from English, French, and Spanish (pp. 156–159) as well as from Caribbean Indian dialects (p. 162). Write students' words and definitions on a chart, then compare them with real words from Creole.

- Make a chart or graph illustrating all the different languages your students and their families use to communicate. Take a larger survey of your school (including staff and teachers) for more data. Use an almanac to compare your findings to language trends in the general population.

Celebrate With Calypso Songs

Jamaican calypso music, or *kaiso* music, as it is known in the Caribbean islands, is popular around the world. This music usually features a strong beat and stories told in authentic Caribbean dialects.

- As you listen to some calypso music, ask students to discern the instruments they hear. Calypso musicians use cowbells, hand clapping, and guiros (gourds etched with ridges, then rubbed with a stick to make a rasping sound), among other instruments. Ask students to identify which instruments convey specific emotions or ideas in the songs.

- Study the words of the calypso included in this book (see p. 167) or those suggested in the Resource Bank (p. 187) or by your music teacher. Read a Caribbean book recommended in the Resource Bank (p. 179). Ask students to help you summarize the book in their own words. Write their interpretations in verse form on chart paper.

- Ask students to use whistles, bells, and homemade drums (pp. 175–176) as they recite their calypso poems. Or, if you have access to a piano, play one of the melodies, substituting kids' words. Display your class poem with Caribbean arts or crafts.

- Play limbo, a dance-game set to calypso music in which players dance beneath a pole (or broomstick or rope) that is lowered with each new round. The winner is the last person to squeeze under the stick without touching it or falling down.

Make a Costume Bank

Important themes in Jonkanoo costumes include horseheads, Indians, fancy ball gowns, devils, butterflies, and Pitchy Patchy figures. (See the sample costume illustrations in the Resource Bank, pp. 130–136.)

- Ask parents and students to comb their attics and thrift stores to find costume decorations. Children can work in small groups to brainstorm sketches for costumes they would like to wear. Allow children to sift through some of the costume materials you have collected to find how to translate their sketches into actual costumes.

- Students can also make puppets from gourds, bags, old socks, and gloves. (See pp. 125 and 127 in the Resource Bank for instructions to make paper-bag puppets and masks.)

Global Awareness

1. Jonkanoo is a mixture of celebrations taken from various cultures—African, Spanish, and British. In your school, home, and community, what examples of cultures borrowing customs from one another do you see?

2. On Trinidad around Christmastime, the high-pitched voices of the *paranderos* can be heard at night as they move from village to village and house to house, celebrating the birth of Christ. They are accompanied by the mandolin, the violin, the rattle of the maraca or *chac chac*, the guitar, and the box base. In many parts of the southwestern United States and in Mexico, the *posada*, or a procession reenacting Joseph and Mary's search for a place to stay in Bethlehem, is held. (*Posada* means "shelter," "lodge," or "inn.") Why, do you think, might these two Christmas festivities have a common Spanish origin?

3. Many children in the United States enjoy watching *The Nutcracker* ballet and Charles Dickens's *A Christmas Carol* during the December holidays. What do these two presentations have in common with holiday celebrations in other parts of the world?

4. Many Jamaicans speak Creole. See the Creole Language Glossary on page 160 for examples of Jamaican Creole.

- In what other countries around the world is some form of Creole spoken?
- How does Creole differ from one group of people to another?

5. Celebrating Jonkanoo was very important to the African slaves in English Caribbean settlements: It was frequently part of the only two "play days" allowed slaves in the traditional twelve holidays of Christmas celebration. At times, denial or restriction of these holidays became a rallying point for slave resistance. What is Labor Day in the United States? When is it celebrated? How is it celebrated? Why is it important?

6. Compare and contrast a contemporary worker in the United States with a Caribbean slave worker: How many hours are there in a work day? What is the type of labor? What are the living conditions? What do workers do on weekends? Are there paid holidays and sick days? Are markets and other kinds of personal shopping available? Is transportation available? Is there easy communication at home and at work? What about recreation and entertainment? Are there job rewards and incentives?

7. Part of Jonkanoo involved the slaves imitating and mimicking their masters. Usually, this was done in fun and not in anger.

- What is a "roast"? Why do people like to mimic those in authority?
- What is a cartoon? What makes it funny?
- Can you find cartoons in the newspaper that make fun of someone in authority? Can you explain them?
- How do you feel about someone mimicking you?

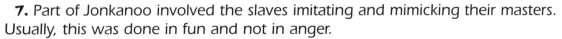

Carnival

Grenada • Martinique • Guadeloupe • Trinidad and Tobago • Haiti • Cuba

Carnival is celebrated on many of the Caribbean islands, but especially those once ruled by France. This holiday was imported by the French settlers who observed it in their native country.

Carnival takes place just before Lent, the time in the Catholic Christian year when people proclaim their devotion to God by giving up things they particularly enjoy or by doing things for others. In a way, Carnival is really the revelers' last chance to have a good time for a while. The day when most of the celebrating takes place is Shrove Tuesday, nicknamed *Fat Tuesday* by Carnivalgoers.

The Monday before Shrove Tuesday is called *Heure Ouvert*, which means "open hour" in French. Islanders pronounced the name of this day *Joovay*, which then became its nickname. Almost everybody belongs to a Joovay club. Joovay members decide on a theme for a loud, colorful act they will perform on the streets. On the day of Carnival, people say, "Play mas!" which means, "Have fun at Carnival!"

Each island has its own style of celebration for this holiday. Trinidad is known for its incredible street performances. People on Grenada especially enjoy making fun of important public figures like politicians and movie stars. On Martinique, Carnival celebrations end when the people burn a huge effigy, or figure, of King Carnival. On all the islands, steel bands keep up a steady beat throughout the festivities. In every celebration, costumes are colorful and wild.

Classroom Enrichment Activities

All Dolled Up

Make madras or gingham dolls in your class to show how the slaves of French plantation houses dressed. Though the custom of dressing in madras, or plaid fabric, began in the eighteenth century, this costume was worn by many women until the 1950s. The headpiece is always made of the same cotton plaid fabric as the dress. When the headpiece is tied, the ends are left loose and fluffy for younger women, and made tighter for older women.

The Egg and You

For Christians, eggs are Easter symbols of new life. During Carnival, people gently crack eggs over one another's heads. Prepare these "smashing" eggs for your Carnival day celebration.

- With a sharp instrument, carefully poke a hole in both ends of an egg. Gently drain or blow out the contents.

- When the egg is completely empty, lightly rinse it out and let dry.

- Use a toothpick to enlarge one of the holes to about the size of a dime.

- Fill the shell with confetti; glue construction paper over the hole.

- Glue bright-colored tissue paper onto the outside of the egg.

- Discuss egg-breaking standards with children before your Carnival celebration.

Make Costumes

Carnival costumes are limitless in terms of style, color, and theme. Use the following suggestions for making basic collars, armbands, and headbands that kids can personalize with feathers, beads, buttons, and paints.

Collars

- Ask students to cut into each paper plate a slit measuring about one fourth of the diameter of the plate, then cut out the inner circle of the plate.

Children can adjust the size of their collars by punching holes in both ends and adding string that can be tied to fit accordingly.

Wristbands

- Cut 7-inch (18-cm) strips of colored or plain oak tag. Students wrap the strips around their wrists and, with the help of partners, make marks showing where they will glue the ends together for a loose fit. (Students need to check that bracelets will fit over one hand when glued.) Students then paste the ends of their oak-tag strips together, let dry, and decorate. Repeat these basic steps to make ankle bands and headbands.

Use some of the sketches of Carnival costumes, found on pages 128–129, for further inspiration.

Carnival Feasts

Invite special guests (parents, other teachers, or members of your Caribbean immigrant community) to small Fête (feast) Parties in which you and your students provide Caribbean foods found in the Resource Bank (see pp. 143–155). During the party, children can present their costumes, sing some calypso selections, and share what they've learned about Carnival with their guests.

It's Instrumental

Have a "mas camp" in your school or classroom. *Mas* is Caribbean for "masquerade." *Camp* refers to the steel drums used to make music. Musical instruments for mas camp bands could include drums (p. 175), "steel" drums, paper plate and bottle-cap cymbals, dried calabash shakers (p. 103), sand blocks (p. 173), and bamboo whistles.

▪ Bring in cookie tins, metal baking sheets, metal hubcaps, and old metal pots or bowls that students can use to experiment with sounds. Students can vary the sounds they make by adding different amounts of water to the pots and bowls or by using materials for drumsticks, such as pencils, plastic rulers, or thick wires.

▪ Ask students to collect materials from junk drawers at home to concoct their own versions of Carnival noisemakers.

▪ Groups of students can work cooperatively to perform some of the calypsos you wrote for Jonkanoo. Help them make a calypso tent (p. 98) in which they can do most of their creative brainstorming, just as calypso composers did in the past.

Spin de Fruit

Make a version of this popular Caribbean Carnival game by following the directions on page 99. Children can take turns playing this game in small groups.

▪ To play, give each child 5–10 pieces of torn paper to use as tokens. Have each child initial his or her pieces. Players each place a token on the fruit to which they think the spinner will point. If the spinner lands on the fruit they chose, they receive an extra token *only if they can answer a trivia question about the Caribbean.* (Use the information in this book or any Caribbean resource to come up with questions, or appoint one student as the "quizzer" for each game.) If the spinner does *not* land on the fruit they chose, the students do not have an opportunity to answer a question.

▪ Each group should have the opportunity to play several rounds. The person who has answered the most Caribbean questions correctly by the end of a predetermined period of time wins.

Global Awareness

Carnival is celebrated all over the world, often at different times of the year. In the United States, Carnival is called Mardi Gras; its biggest celebration takes place in New Orleans, Louisiana. Other huge celebrations are held in September in Brooklyn, New York, and right after Easter in San Francisco, California.

1. What kind of carnivals have you attended? Where were they held? Who was there? Was anyone in costume? Was there a parade, special music, or special foods? Did children have a special role?

2. The steelpan is the only musical instrument invented in the twentieth century. In 1992 it was declared the national instrument of Trinidad and Tobago. Find out more about the origins of this instrument.

3. *Carnival* comes from the Latin word *carnelevare* which means "to take meat away." After Carnival, people would eat meatless meals.

- What nutrient does meat provide in our diet?

- What other foods provide this nutrient?

- Are there any meatless Caribbean recipes you could make that would provide adequate amounts of this nutrient? (See the Resource Bank, pp. 143–155.)

4. Find out more about Carnival by using resources in the library.

- Where else in the world is Carnival celebrated?

- Are the festivities the same everywhere? For example, is the length of the celebration the same everywhere? Where do the celebrations take place—indoors or outdoors? When in the year are they held?

Rara

Haiti

Rara is a big festival held in Haiti every year at the time of the Christian season of Lent. It takes place on the weekends during Lent and started as a revolt against Catholicism during the holiday of Carnival, which is held just before Lent. (See page 52 for more on Carnival). The word *rara* means "noise" in Haitian. Revelers "make rara" with shrill whistles, hooting bamboo vaccines, thumping drums, raucous singing, and hip-twisting dancing.

In Rara festivities, ancient African religious practices, including voodoo, are mixed with Caribbean folk traditions and Catholic traditions that slaves adopted from plantation owners. *Voodoo*, or *vodoun*, means "spirit" or "deity" and came from the West African Yoruba religion. Many of the words used in voodoo rituals are a mixture of French and African. Among the voodoo gods are Legba (god of the crossroads), Ogun (god of war), Agoure (god of the seas), Baron Samidi (god of the dead spirits), Agoue (a fishlike god), and the god St. James, dressed in his armor. Gods eat, drink, fuss, and fall in love—sort of like humans but on a grander scale. Voodoo practices vary from village to village. For a long time, voodoo was against the law in Haiti, but in 1995 the Haitian government declared that it could be legally practiced.

On the day after Ash Wednesday, bands of Rara revelers set fire to Carnival symbols such as masks and costumes. Celebrators trace their fingers in the ashes and draw crosses on their foreheads. Animals or other possessions are often sacrificed. Symbols of gods are drawn on the ground with products grown on the island, such as flour, sugar, cornmeal, and coffee. Rara parades are led by flag bearers, with two or more major joncs twirling batons. Joncs are symbolic and do magical maneuvers. In each parade are also a queen and her attendants, a musical ensemble, a women's choir, and women vendors who sell refreshments.

Classroom Enrichment Activities

Plan a Rara Parade

Make some Rara costumes for a parade. (See the Resource Bank for jonc tunics and headpieces, pp. 137–138). Costumes could be constructed out of tinsel, beads, scarves, and other colored cloth.

Major Jonc, a Rara character, always wears a cape of honor on which are fastened many glittering decorations. Part of his costume also includes short pants, a shirt, and a tunic.

The Rara queen and her attendants wear long, bright-colored dresses of fancy fabric like taffeta or rayon, and elaborate jeweled headwraps or broad-brimmed hats decorated with cloth strips in various colors. Gloved and adorned with many baubles, women often wear skirts that reveal ruffled petticoats under them.

Zulu Ankle Rattles

Something to add to Rara costumes are ankle rattles, just as the Zulus did. These rattles made a loud rhythmic sound as the people danced. (See the Resource Bank, p. 174.)

Make Flags

Make some flags for your Rara parade or just to display with reports about Haiti or the Caribbean. Discuss some of the gods celebrated during this festival. Ask students to think of some symbols that would represent each Yoruba god's role. For instance, Agoue, the fish god, might be represented with fish and sea symbols. After students have decided which symbols they will use, help them use white glue to create their designs on black paper; sprinkle designs with cornmeal, sugar, coffee, or flour as you would use glitter. Let dry, then shake off the excess to see the designs clearly.

Host a Haitian Visitor

If possible, invite people with a Haitian background to come to the class and share their heritage with your students.

▪ Have students prepare well-researched questions beforehand to ask their visitors. Possible questions could include

What are some traditions of Rara that are always observed?

Are there special Rara foods?

▪ Take some time to teach your children some French words to use in greeting and speaking to your Haitian visitor(s). See the French Language glossary on page 156 for help.

© 1997 Fearon Teacher Aids

Global Awareness

The island of Hispaniola, about half the size of Cuba, is occupied by two separate nations: Haiti and the Dominican Republic. Haiti is the smaller of the two countries. Most Haitians are of African descent, but their culture is a mixture of African and French.

1. In 1804 a group of black slaves massacred, or killed, most of the French colonial landowners. The slaves were led by Toussaint L'Ouverture. What qualities made him a good leader? Compare him with other people who led a fight for equal rights (such as Martin Luther King, Jr. or Nelson Mandela).

2. Are there peoples in the world today who are still fighting for equal rights or humanitarian treatment? Where are they located? Who are they fighting against? What are their chief complaints?

3. Today the African cult of *vodoun* (voodoo) plays an important part in everyday Haitian life. Records of Rara festivals go all the way back to the French colonial period. On New Year's Eve a group of slaves would dress up and appear before their masters to collect gifts in long-handled baskets. Compare this to a holiday that is celebrated in the United States.

4. How are Halloween and Rara similar? What Christian religious day takes place just after Halloween? Why, do you think, do the Haitian people participate in Rara?

5. African music and Rara music have become popular with many people around the world.

- What makes Rara music different from other kinds of music?
- What kinds of instruments are used?

6. Where do most of the people live in Haiti—in the countryside or in the cities? Why? Find out what is available in Haitian markets for people to buy.

Native People's Week

All Islands

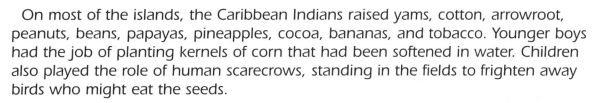

Amerindian tribes like the Tainos, Ciboneys, Arawaks, and Caribs were the first people we are aware of who lived on the Caribbean islands. They probably came from South America in dugout canoes thousands of years ago. We call them pre-Columbian peoples because they lived here long before Columbus "discovered" the region. Archeologists know about them from finding remains of their pottery, living sites, and rock art.

One of the things these early Caribbeans brought with them from South America was the manioc tree, which they planted all over the islands in mounds so the roots wouldn't be burned by the intense sunlight. These roots, called cassava, were valuable; they could be ground into a flour to make bread. After the flour was turned into dough, it was formed into loaves and cooked on clay griddles over an open fire.

On most of the islands, the Caribbean Indians raised yams, cotton, arrowroot, peanuts, beans, papayas, pineapples, cocoa, bananas, and tobacco. Younger boys had the job of planting kernels of corn that had been softened in water. Children also played the role of human scarecrows, standing in the fields to frighten away birds who might eat the seeds.

Besides farming, the Caribbean Indians also got their food from the sea. They found mussels and oysters among the roots of the mangrove trees and conchs in the deeper waters. They carved decoys, or realistic statues, from dried gourds, then set them on the rivers and lakes to attract and trap ducks. The Amerindians used tamed parrots to attract wild parrots, which they captured and cooked as a special treat.

The Amerindians lived in family groups that included grandmothers, grandfathers, aunts, uncles, and cousins. The oldest son of the oldest sister in a tribe was the cacique, or chief. Each tribe had its own set of rules.

Amerindians believed that the world was run by magic and that a god called Yaya was its mythical father. They also believed in other gods. Iochu was the giver of food; a fertility goddess helped people have children; and a third god took care of the dead. Early settlers and explorers were shocked to discover that the Caribs were cannibals, or eaters of human flesh. Europeans had a hard time understanding that this ritual was a part of the Carib religion.

Many Amerindians were killed by diseases brought to the islands by the white men and the African slaves. Amerindians were also made slaves by their conquerors. There are no more full-blooded native Caribbean people left, but many of the islands hold a Native People's Week each year to honor the contributions and memory of these ancient islanders.

Classroom Enrichment Activities

Amazing Maize

Read some stories about the origins of maize, or corn (see the Bibliography of Resources for Kids, p. 179). It's believed that Carib Indians brought this vegetable with them when they migrated from South America.

- Bring in a variety of ears of corn—white, yellow, bicolor, red, blue. Point out that the kind of corn sold in stores today is much different from the ancient varieties. Let students touch, smell, and taste the corn when it is boiled, steamed in its husk, or dried and grated to form a coarse powder.

- Make Cornmeal Cou Cou (p. 152).

- Ask students to brainstorm as many corn dishes as they can from their own cultural heritage.

Try Some Dye

Europeans who first visited the Caribbean islands were often shocked at how many tattoos, or body paintings, the Amerindians wore. People used a plant called *roc* to produce a bright red dye and onion skins to make a yellowish dye. Village priests blackened their faces with charcoal.

- Experiment with vegetable dyes. Ask students to brainstorm some natural materials that could be used to produce specific colors. Place vegetables or fruits, with a splash of vinegar to make the colors stronger, in a small pan of water, and boil for about 30 minutes. When each solution has cooled, test colors on white chart paper. (You can refrigerate solutions before testing if necessary.) Ask students to use their observations about the colors the different materials produced to brainstorm even more sources for natural dyes. (See also p. 112 in the Resource Bank for another dye-making project.)

- Ask students to design tattoo symbols that would have been appropriate for people with customs and religious beliefs similar to those of the native Caribbean people. Symbols should be taken primarily from nature, incorporating the foliage, animal life, and environmental themes of an island population. Because the vegetable dyes you made may not be strong enough to color these drawings, ask children to use watercolors in natural shades.

Make a Wiss Vine Basket

The Amerindians were skilled at weaving baskets and other household items. Make a basket like one they would have made, using softened reed. See the Resource Bank, page 101, for directions.

Have a Native People's Party

Serve pepper pot and other foods listed in the Resource Bank (p. 150). Decorate the classroom with Caribbean paper flowers (pp. 83–84), tattoo sketches, dried gourds, and wiss vine baskets.

Global Awareness

1. The Amerindians used grinding stones to make cassava bread, one of their most important foods. What was the primary occupation of the Native Americans who once lived in *your* area? What was their main staple of food? How did they obtain and prepare it?

2. The Arawaks introduced many fruits and vegetables from South America, including cashew nuts, pineapples, red peppers, and avocados. What were some of the fruits, vegetables, and wild game the North American Indians introduced to the new settlers in their area? What did the Indians contribute to the first Thanksgiving feast?

3. The Arawaks used stone instruments to carve rock drawings or petroglyphs on large boulders. Are there ancient petroglyphs in your area? Do you know what they mean?

4. To make canoes, the Tainos hollowed out dead tree trunks with hot coals. What kind of transportation did the Native Americans in your area use? How was it constructed? What materials did they use?

5. Daniel DeFoe wrote *Robinson Crusoe* in 1719–1720, based on the true life story of Alexander Selkirk. In the book, Crusoe is a shipwrecked sailor who spends 24 years on a deserted island. He eventually meets a young Arawak whom he saves from death at the hands of some Carib cannibals. Do you know of any legends or true stories about native people in your area?

Crop Over

Barbados • Trinidad

The sugar-cane growing season is long; it can take a full year for a crop to reach maturity. Many Bajans and Trinidadians throw a big party after the harvest, when a new batch of sugar cane has been cut.

This celebration, called Crop Over, may have been started by plantation owners to reward slaves for bringing in the sugar cane. In 1788 the owner of Newton Plantation on Barbados gave "a dinner and sober dance" for his slaves after a particularly good harvest. This is the first mention of what later became the Crop Over festival.

To get ready for the beginning of the festival, Bajans elect a Crop Over king and queen. One year the Crop Over queen was a woman who loaded 513 pounds (230 kg) of sugar cane in one season!

Carts carrying the last cane stalks of the season are decorated with colorful frangipani flowers and moss. Women marching in the parade balance elaborately decorated baskets filled with colorful fruits on their heads.

A huge effigy, or life-size doll, of a mysterious character called Mr. Harding is presented to the manager of the sugar mill. Supposedly, Mr. Harding represents the hardships endured during a growing season. The figure is burned to say goodbye to those difficult times.

One of the foods enjoyed during this festival is soursop punch, made from a dark green, pine-cone-shaped fruit that grows on the island. Archaeologists believe that this plant has been a part of the islanders' diets since long before Europeans arrived.

Classroom Enrichment Activities

Salute to Sugar

Explain to children the basic steps of processing sugar cane, listed in the section on Barbados (see p. 16).

- Many specialty grocery stores now stock sugar cane, so try bringing some in for children to sample. (You'll need a very sharp, heavy-duty knife to cut open the cane for children to suck on.) Also provide molasses, brown sugar, honey, corn syrup, and refined (white) sugar for students to taste, smell, and touch.

- Make an attribute chart with pictures of each sweetener across the top. List in the appropriate column some of the adjectives that children think of to describe each one.

- Ask children to collect labels from their favorite foods; supplement labels that children provide with some that show *low* sugar content. Read and discuss ingredients listed on labels. (Point out that ingredients are listed in order from greatest amount to least amount.)

- Make a large graph showing foods with a range of sugar content. Look at a food pyramid and talk about where sugar fits in a healthy diet.

- Make a box theater (see p. 96 for directions) for children to show "movies" about the sugar process and other sugar-related facts.

Crown Your Queens and Kings

- Divide students into pairs. Ask children to make lists of reasons why their partners deserve to become queens or kings of the Crop Over festival. Children can make up reasons to crown one another based on what they've learned about Bajan culture, as well as personal accomplishments or qualities of their partners. For instance, they might list as reasons: *Susie chopped 300 stalks of cane* or *Nori always shares.*

- Ask students to use oak tag to make crowns for one another, adding Caribbean and sugar-cane-related scenes for decoration. During a special crowning ceremony, partners can present each other as queens or kings and read aloud their lists of royal attributes. Children can also wear their courtly regalia in your Crop Over parade.

Have a Crop Over Parade

- Help children use tissue paper and paint to turn large cardboard boxes or smaller matchboxes into colorful flower-covered "cane carts," then add string for pulling the creations in the Crop Over parade. (See illustrations on p. 64 and construction directions on p. 107.)

- Students can make Barbados flags to wave in the parade (see p. 177), sing a Hosanna (p. 167), and play instruments used in the Caribbean, including drums, gourd maracas, tambourines, and simple guitars made from tissue boxes and rubber bands (see Index, p. 192). Have students research the flag's colors using library, CD-ROM, or Internet resources.

Here is a cart you might see during a Crop Over parade in Barbados.

The back of the cart is lavishly decorated.

Make Bajan Food

One food commonly found in Barbados is the coconut. In fact, it's so common that you might find many bits of shell and husk while walking on the beach there.

The coconut palm can grow up to 50 feet (15 m) tall. The fruit itself may be as much as 1 foot (30 cm) long and almost as wide. People sometimes use the strong fibers of the fruit's outer husk to make rope and coarse cloth.

If you crack a coconut shell open, you'll find the soft white "meat" of the fruit as well as the opaque liquid called the milk. Dried coconut meat is called copra. The oil is used in making soap, candles, and a common food additive used as a softening agent. (This oil is extremely high in fat!)

- Give children the opportunity to sample the sweet, piquant taste of coconut by making Coconut Rice (see p. 144). Then help them appreciate the Bajan spices used to make Caribbean Carrot Sticks (p. 144) and Bajan Cakes (see Recipes, p. 155).

- Make a coconut-shaped theme book to tell all about the coconut, such as where it grows, how it's harvested, its many uses, and other things learned about the marvelous coconut (see pp. 80–81).

Stage a Cohobblopot Show

A cohobblopot is used in Barbados to cook a variety of foods; a cohobblopot show is similar to a variety, or talent, show during which participants present their special skills or knowledge.

- For your cohobblopot show, help students prepare something they've learned about Barbados in any way they choose—by writing a poem, story, or song, playing musical instruments, or performing a skit.

- You may want to present the show to other classes on Kadooment Day, a national holiday in Barbados and the final day of the Crop Over festival.

© 1997 Fearon Teacher Aids

Global Awareness

1. Sugar cane is still the main crop on Barbados even though fewer acres are planted now than in past years.

- Do you live in an area where there is one main crop or product?
- What is it and how is it grown and harvested?

2. Find out where sugar cane is grown in the United States. How is it planted? What is meant by "holing"? What other crop is grown in the United States to produce sugar? Compare these two crops.

3. The sugar-cane harvest once continued for six to eight months, but today harvesting often takes place throughout the year. Harvesting and milling the ripe sugar cane is hard work, so a celebration is often held after these tasks are completed. Do you know of any local festivals where harvests are celebrated in your area? (For instance, apples in Washington, grapes in California, corn in Kansas, peanuts in Georgia.)

4. In colonial times, life on the Bajan plantations was like life on plantations in Virginia and other southern American colonies.

- Why were they so much alike? How were they different?
- Why were Africans used for labor in both regions?

5. Are there festivities like Crop Over held in other parts of the world to celebrate the harvesting of a major crop? What are these festivities like? What are the festivities called?

6. Sometimes people will work a patch of sugar cane for the owner of the land for a share of the profits. These people who farm part of another person's land are called sharecroppers.

- What crops do sharecroppers raise in the United States?
- Why, do you think, do they do this?

Regatta

St. Vincent and the Grenadines •
British Virgin Islands • Grenada

Regatta is a time to celebrate boating, beaches, the ocean, and all kinds of watersports. Regattas are boat races between boats of the same class, or size and type. For instance, during Regatta season (usually in the summertime), people sail, watch the races, or just enjoy the festivities that surround this occasion.

Early Caribbean peoples made canoes from hollowed logs; oars were carved from thick green branches that were smoked, or seasoned, to make them even stronger. The oarsmen moved a boat by slicing the oars through the water much as fins move a fish. Canoes were very important to native Caribbeans because they used them to trade with South American tribes.

Early sailing vessels had square sails. After that came lantees, big, boxy boats with triangular sails. Around the time of Columbus, sailing ships were becoming faster and more powerful. Boat makers were highly skilled artisans. They began to carve the bodies, or hulls, of ships in the shapes of graceful fish. They found new ways to attach the sails of these vessels to their masts so that they could move at greater speeds with less wind power.

As settlements on Caribbean islands grew, different types of boats filled the harbors. There were slave ships (see illustration on p. 4), tall sailing ships for longer voyages, and Manila galleons (p. 35), which were used mostly for trading.

Today, you can find huge cruise ships parked a mile off the coasts of different islands; rowboats, plastic kayaks, and motorboats puttering around the bays and inlets; and sailboats and reproductions of old schooners that people still use for show and racing.

Regatta

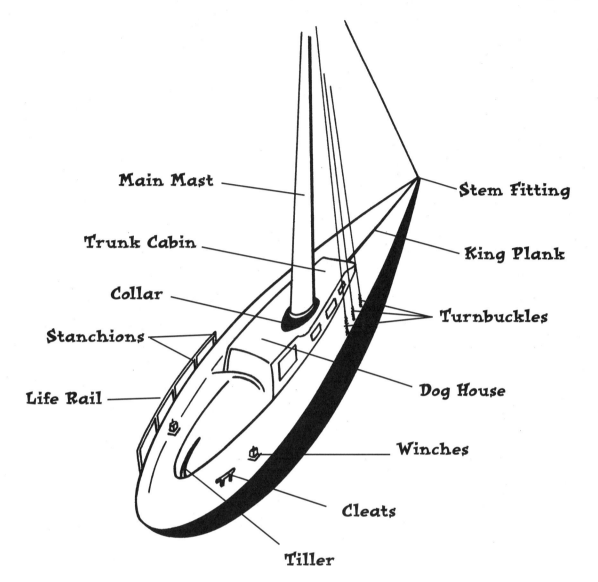

Main Mast

Stem Fitting

Trunk Cabin

King Plank

Collar

Turnbuckles

Stanchions

Life Rail

Dog House

Winches

Cleats

Tiller

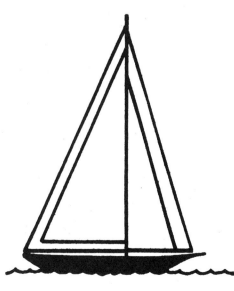

Classroom Enrichment Activities

Boating Safety

Bring in pictures of ships and boats of all sorts from magazines and newspapers. Hold a poster contest in which students think of as many rules for safe boating as possible. Ask a sailing specialist in your community to be one of the judges.

Ship's Logs

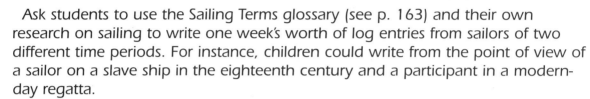

Ask students to use the Sailing Terms glossary (see p. 163) and their own research on sailing to write one week's worth of log entries from sailors of two different time periods. For instance, children could write from the point of view of a sailor on a slave ship in the eighteenth century and a participant in a modern-day regatta.

Knot Tying

Any good sailor learns to tie knots well, for there are many times that boats must be securely tied. Also in the handling of boat equipment such as the sails, knot tying is a vital skill. Practice tying some simple knots (see p. 118 in the Resource Bank). For an added challenge, research library resources to find more difficult knots to tie.

Matchbox Boats

Ask parents to help you collect matchboxes and other small boxes to transform into boats. Students can make models based on their favorite boats and add them to shoebox dioramas depicting Caribbean scenes or use them in a boat race. (See p. 119 in the Resource Bank.)

Breadfruit Barbecue

Barbecue breadfruit for a beach bash at Regatta time. Roast breadfruit for an hour over hot coals. Turn three or four times. When steam starts to escape, the breadfruit is done. Remove from fire, cut off the end, and scoop out the heart and toss it out. Remove the burned outer skin, slice the breadfruit, and serve hot.

Global Awareness

Cruising, racing, sailing, snorkeling, scuba diving, fishing, shell seeking, and treasure hunting are just a few ways to celebrate the sea during Regatta.

1. The Caribbean Sea has a different color from the Atlantic Ocean and is often much calmer.

- What do sailors mean when they call the direction of the wind windward or leeward?

- What are trade winds?

- Why were trade winds important to Christopher Columbus?

- What are hurricanes? What causes them?

2. Even though whaling is outlawed in many places, fishermen are still allowed to harpoon whales from February to May on the island of Bequia. Many places in the United States were once whaling centers but are now mainly used for whale watching when the whales migrate to their breeding grounds. What can you discover about some of these old whaling ports?

3. Ancient Caribbean coral reefs provide great fascination for people who come from around the world to snorkel and scuba dive.

- How is snorkeling different from scuba diving?

- Where in the United States have you seen or done some of these interesting seashore activities?

4. Ship captains use flags with international symbols to provide identification of their ships and to send short messages to other seagoing ships. Sometimes the flags are used to dress a ship for ceremonial or festive occasions. Find out what these nautical, or marine, flags look like and how they are used.

5. Shell collecting is a fun thing to do in the Caribbean because of the many islands' beaches. Lots of shells can be found there. Why is it important to find out if there are any rules to follow when looking for and collecting shells?

San Juan's Day

Puerto Rico

San Juan's Day, June 24, is the day of the patron saint, John the Baptizer. The island of Puerto Rico was first named San Juan Bautista. When it was renamed Puerto Rico, or Rich Port, San Juan became the name of the capital city.

The Coat of Arms of Puerto Rico was given to the island by King Ferdinand and Queen Isabella. Ferdinand came from the Lion, or Leon family, so a symbol of a lion is included on the crest. Isabella came from the Castle, or Castillo family. Symbols of castles are shown on the crest to represent Isabella. The cross is a symbol for Christianity.

San Juan's Day is celebrated with festive food and a procession. In the morning, people prepare picnics or dinners to eat on the beach. At 6:00 P.M., the celebrants walk to the seashore. All night long there are barbecues and bonfires at the beach. At midnight the young and old alike jump into the water. They turn around three times toward the shore, three times toward the sea, and then walk backward out of the sea. This is considered magical and will wash evil spirits away.

On San Juan's Day, there is always a holiday market with fruits, vegetables, candies, and little trinkets for sale. These include cornhusk dolls, shell boxes (p. 91), gold bracelets (p. 107), seed beads (p. 105), and other art pieces (pp. 122 and 124) made by the children.

Classroom Enrichment Activities

Music, Music, Music

Be on the lookout for Puerto Rican recordings, tapes, and CDs perhaps with music of the salsa, mambo, and merengue.

■ Enlist the help of your school or district music and PE specialists to find examples of these and other "spicy" rhythms and teach the dances to your girls and boys for your San Juan's Day party.

■ Your own class orchestra can keep the beat with instruments they made or brought into class. Be sure they are adding to the music by keeping the beat and not just making noise.

■ Share with students a recording by the great cellist Pablo Casals, a Puerto Rican. This is music appreciation at its best.

Class Coat of Arms

Design a coat of arms for your class. Transfer the design to flags, cardboard shields, or paper crests, and add these to your Caribbean display. To get started, look at Puerto Rico's (p. 70) and Jamaica's (p. 115) coat of arms. Then ask small groups of children to brainstorm ideas or objects to include on a class shield or coat of arms.

■ For example, what is the name of your town or city? Is the town or city famous for something? If so, what is it famous for?

■ What are students' three favorite activities?

■ What is the class's favorite animal?

■ Does your area get a lot of one type of weather, such as snow, rain, or sunshine?

■ What is the topography of the land where you live? Are there mountains, flat plains, farmlands, lakes, cities with skyscrapers, or other kinds of unique features? Can you think of a symbol (or symbols) to show this topography?

Another option would be to create classroom stories from the coats of arms and input the stories or legends into the computer. Set the texts with a font or typeface that makes the lettering look as if it came from the fifteenth century, then print out the stories and stain the papers with an instant-aging solution of cooled strong tea or coffee, sponged gently over the documents.

Global Awareness

An important holiday in most parts of Puerto Rico is San Juan's Day, on June 24. This is the feast of Saint John the Baptizer and is observed in many places throughout the world. It also occurs around the time of Midsummer's Day, which has been celebrated since pre-Christian times. Midsummer's Day is also called the summer solstice.

1. San Juan, the capital of Puerto Rico, was founded and named to honor Saint John the Baptizer. Much of the old town either remains or has been restored. Today you can visit the home where Juan Ponce de León lived when he was Governor General of Puerto Rico.

- Why is Ponce de León important in North American history?

- What mythical treasure was he looking for?

2. John is one of the most popular of all names given to boys. In many Latin countries, including those where Spanish is the first language, people celebrate not only the date of their birth but also the festival of the saint they were named after; this is called one's name day. So everybody in Puerto Rico named Juan or John celebrates on the twenty-fourth of June.

- What are the most popular names in your class for boys and for girls?

- What holiday would you declare for your name day?

3. San Juan's Day in Puerto Rico is a popular holiday and family day when many people do not have to go to work. Instead, they go to the beach for food, music, and fun. In the United States we celebrate our nation's birthday on the Fourth of July; does it remind you a little of this Caribbean holiday? Why or why not?

© 1997 Fearon Teacher Aids

Section 3

Resource Bank

Arts and Crafts
Sample Leaf Patterns

Provide the following leaf patterns (enlarge as needed) for children to use to create their own classroom rain forest.

On the long, smooth-sided leaf (like a peach leaf), use the backside of a scissors blade and make a long crease mark down the center of the leaf. This will give the leaf a bit of shape.

Shaped Leaves

Paper sculpture can be applied to leaves. Then curl leaf sections to make them appear three-dimensional. To curl paper, use a closed pair of scissors and pull the leaf across the scissors' flat edge or pull a larger leaf back and forth across the edge of a table.

Miniature Rain Forest

Before you set up this experiment, ask children to predict what they think will happen. Using their knowledge of the Caribbean rain forest, they can determine what the lid or plastic wrap represents (the different layers of rain-forest growth). As the "rain forest" grows, ask children to keep a journal of observations about this terrarium experiment.

Materials

- wide-mouth jar and lid or plastic wrap
- gravel
- planting soil
- small plants such as moss and ferns, or tropical plant seeds like bougainvillea or hibiscus
- water

1. Place a layer of gravel in the bottom of the jar.
2. Add about 2 inches (5 cm) soil.
3. Add plants or seeds.
4. Sprinkle plants or soil with water (about 1/4 cup, or 60 ml, for a jar that's 6 inches, or 15 cm, wide).
5. Place the lid or plastic wrap loosely over the jar.
6. Keep the jar in a warm place away from direct sunlight.

Crayon-Resist Caribbean Sea Murals

Children will enjoy making either crayon-resist murals or pictures (see activity below). To prepare for this activity, have groups of children research some of the plants and animals that live in Caribbean waters. Then help students follow the simple steps below to make crayon-resist murals.

Materials

- mural paper
- pencil
- colorful wax crayons
- newspaper
- blue, green, and brown watercolors
- wide paintbrushes

1. Spread very large sheets of mural paper on the floor.

2. Use pencil to sketch an ocean scene of sea plants and animals.

3. Trace over the pencil sketch with crayon; make sure to press very hard so that the outlines of objects really stand out.

4. Protect the floor with newspaper.

5. Paint over the crayon scene with blue, green, and brown watercolors to create an ocean effect.

6. After the murals have dried, hang them all around the room.

Crayon-Resist Pictures

Ask children to think of various Caribbean items to include in a crayon-resist picture. Items such as fish, shells, seaweed, and jellyfish could be used for a Regatta or Native People's Week celebration; or sugar cane, coconuts, banana trees, pineapple plants, and the like could be drawn for a Crop Over festival in Barbados.

Materials

- pencils
- sturdy drawing paper
- wax crayons in an assortment of vivid colors
- watercolor paints
- wide brushes or sponges

1. Design a picture using items associated with a particular festival.

2. Draw the design on the paper.

3. Generously color in the design with bright wax crayons.

4. Use the watercolor paints to put a wash over the drawing. (Sponges or wide brushes work best for this.)

5. Where the wax is heaviest, the paper will resist the paint. Where the wax is thin, more paint will show on the paper.

Sand Casting

Materials

- fine sand
- beach items: shells, dried seaweed, driftwood, sea glass
- milk cartons of various sizes, tops cut off
- plaster of Paris mix
- water
- digging tools

1. Fill carton with sand and thoroughly moisten sand.
2. Place hand in sand to make a firm hole about 2 inches (5 cm) deep.
3. Embed some natural beach items in the sand on the sides and bottom of the hole.
4. Prepare plaster of Paris and carefully pour it into the still-damp sand hole.
5. Let dry for 24 hours (or according to package directions).
6. Carefully lift plaster cast from mold and shake off excess sand.

Sand Candles

Materials

- milk carton, top cut off
- fine sand
- melted candle wax
- wick
- water

1. Fill carton with damp sand and create a deep hole by hand.
2. Fasten a small stick or paper clip on the end of a wick. Bury the clip or stick in the bottom of the hole.
3. Pour melted wax into the hole while holding wick upright.
4. Allow wax to harden overnight. Peel away paper carton and wipe loose sand away. Trim excess wick off candle bottom.

Sand Castles

Materials

- sand tables or newspaper
- plastic sheets or large garbage bags
- fine sand
- water
- diluted white glue (about 1 part glue to 15 parts water)
- digging tools
- spray bottle

1. Set up a work area using a sand table or thin stacks of newspaper and the plastic sheeting or garbage bags.

2. Place a small pile of sand in the work area and soak with water. Pile on more sand and wet again with water.

3. Dig away the wet sand to expose the "hidden" castle.

4. To keep the sculpted areas wet, use the spray bottle containing the diluted white glue to spray the castle. Use as needed to help the castle hold its shape.

Sand Painting

Materials

- fine sand
- powdered tempera paint
- sketch paper
- crayons or markers
- plywood or masonite in a variety of shapes
- white glue, slightly diluted
- paintbrushes of various sizes and shapes

1. Mix small quantities of sand with tempera powder in Caribbean colors like blue, green, yellow, and tan.

2. Draw and color a feature of one of the Caribbean islands on sketch paper.

3. Transfer the picture to the plywood or masonite.

4. Paint one area of the picture with diluted glue mixture and sprinkle it with one color of sand.

5. Allow the glue to dry; dump excess sand back into the proper container.

6. Repeat the last two steps until you have used all the colors you desire.

Volcano

Materials

- 16-ounce (480-ml) soda bottle, rinsed and dried
- large board
- chicken wire
- papier-mâché strips and paste
- plaster of Paris (optional)
- 1 tablespoon (15 ml) flour
- 1 tablespoon (15 ml) baking soda
- spoon
- 2 measuring cups
- funnel
- red food coloring
- 1 cup (240 ml) white vinegar
- tap water to clean up

To Make the Volcano

1. Place the soda bottle in the center of a large board.
2. Shape chicken wire around the bottle to make a cone. Be sure to leave the bottle opening uncovered.
3. Tack the wire to the board.
4. Cover the wire with strips of papier-mâché to form a "mountain" cone.
5. Dribble plaster of Paris down the sides of the finished cone to suggest lava deposits.

To Make the Volcano Erupt

1. Mix the flour and baking soda together in one of the measuring cups.
2. Use the funnel to pour the mixture into the bottle opening in your volcano.
3. Add 20 drops of the food coloring to the bottle.
4. Pour vinegar into the second measuring cup to equal 1 cup. Carefully pour about half of the vinegar into the bottle.
5. When the foaming stops, pour the rest of the vinegar into the bottle and watch as the volcano oozes "lava."

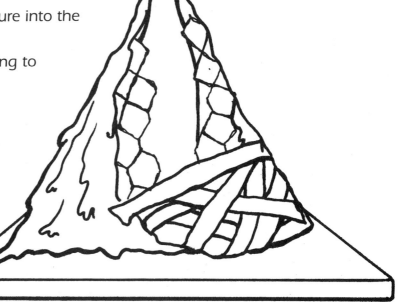

Shape or Theme Books

For a short story that has a major theme, such as how pineapple, sugar cane, or coconut grows, pages can be prepared so they suggest the topic of the story by the shape of the cover. The cover can have an elaborate or simple design. (See below and p. 81 for ideas.) To bind the pages into a booklet, a long-arm stapler or a saddle stapler works best.

Materials

- writing paper or plain newsprint
- construction paper
- stapler
- pencils, pens
- sharp scissors
- markers

1. Fold a few sheets of writing paper in half (three sheets will make six pages, which is a good amount).

2. Fold a sheet of construction paper around the folded writing paper to form a booklet, with the folded edges together.

3. Hold the papers together, open the booklet to the center pages, and staple (from the outside in) along the fold, or the spine. This will help hold the pages together as you cut out the book shape.

4. Draw the desired shape of the book on the front cover (see sample designs to the right and on p. 81).

5. Cut out the shape, cutting through all pages.

6. Write the story inside.

7. If desired, draw a decorative design on the front cover to highlight the book's theme. Include the book's title at the top, then fill in the design with colorful markers.

THE STORY OF PINEAPPLE PLANTATIONS

THOSE GIANT PLANTS!

Shape or Theme Books

THE STORY OF THE SUGAR CANE BUSINESS

TREES OF THE CARIBBEAN

The FISHIEST STORY

STEEL DRUM STORY

PIRATE COVE TALE

Flowers

cattleya orchid

frangipani (Plumeria)

bottle brush tree

ginger

hibiscus

bougainvillea

Frangipani (Plumeria)

This five-petal flower is extremely fragrant. Its colors are usually pastel, however, it can be seen occasionally in deeper pinks and an almost reddish color.

Materials

- pencils
- flower pattern (see below)
- construction paper in pastel colors
- scissors
- tape or floral tape
- wire

1. Draw frangipani flower forms on colorful construction paper, using the pattern below. Cut out.

2. With closed scissors, curl each petal away from you. [diagram A]

3. Roll the stem of the flower so that petal A and petal B meet.

4. Tape the rolled stem together and add wire (with tape) to form a longer stem. [diagram B]

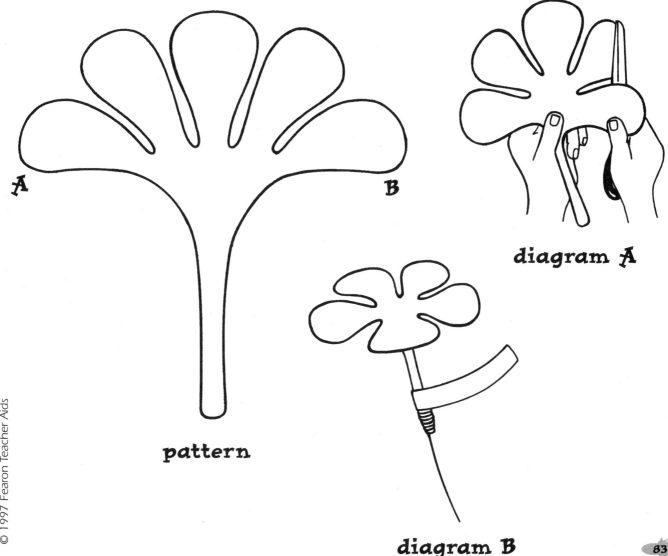

A   B

diagram A

pattern

diagram B

Bougainvillea

These woody vines have thousands of blossoms, which provide a showy mass of color.

Materials

- construction paper in brilliant colors like fuschia, orange, pink, red, yellow
- pattern (see below)
- pencils
- scissors
- tape or glue
- wire

1. Trace and cut out three petals using the pattern below.

2. Fold each petal in half lengthwise to create a crease, then unfold.

3. Using closed scissors, curl the top part of each petal away from the fold. [diagram A]

4. Tape or glue the uncurled sides of the petals together, with the outside part of the fold facing in to the center of the flower.

5. Make a stamen, using several strands of wire. Leave top 1 1/2 inches (3.75 cm) free and twist wire below to form a stem. [diagram B]

6. Insert stamen in the middle of the flower and tape or glue in place.

7. Twist the stems of several flowers together.

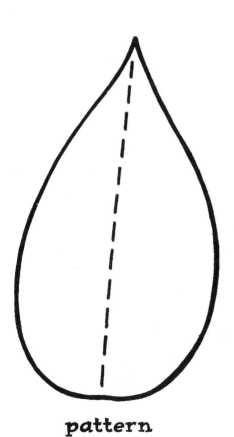

pattern

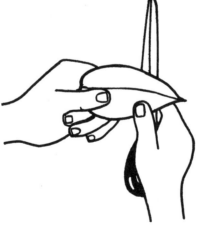

diagram A

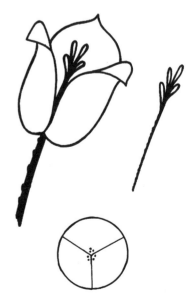

diagram B

Fish

Encourage students to research the following and other Caribbean fishes to learn more about each, such as its size, diet, and habitat. Fish facts could be included on fish flags or fish mobiles.

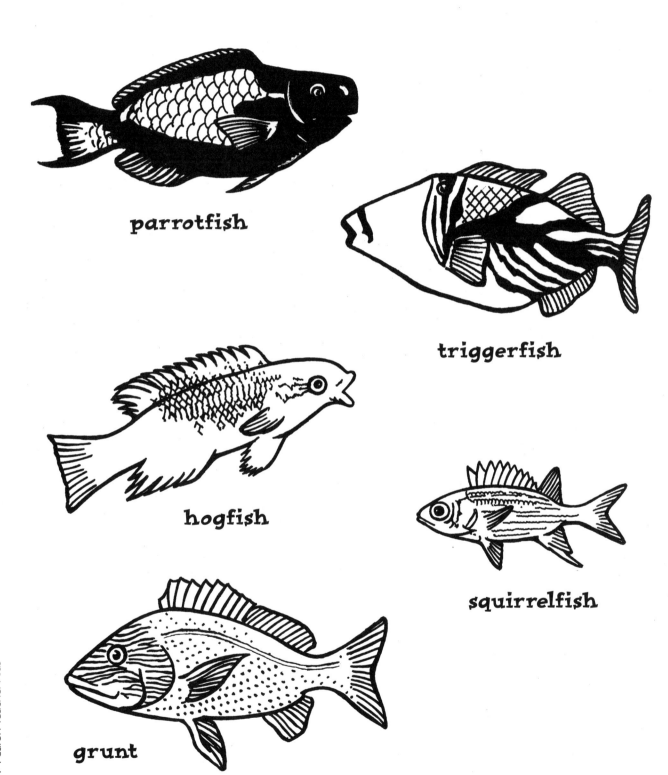

parrotfish

triggerfish

hogfish

squirrelfish

grunt

whitetip shark

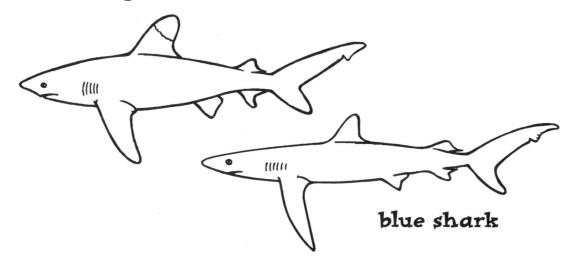

blue shark

great barracuda

southern stingray   **spotted eagle ray**

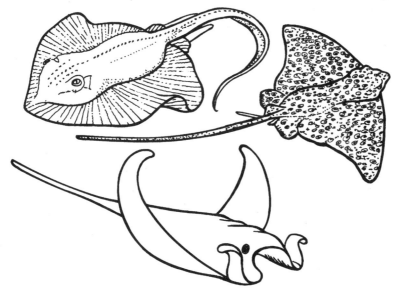

Atlantic manta

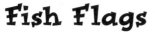

Fish Flags

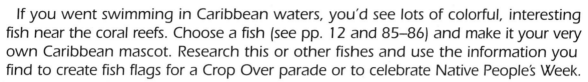

If you went swimming in Caribbean waters, you'd see lots of colorful, interesting fish near the coral reefs. Choose a fish (see pp. 12 and 85–86) and make it your very own Caribbean mascot. Research this or other fishes and use the information you find to create fish flags for a Crop Over parade or to celebrate Native People's Week.

Materials

- pencils
- butcher paper or grocery bags
- scissors
- staplers
- scrunchable scrap paper (for stuffing material)

- tempera paint and paintbrushes
- hole punch
- yarn
- thin wooden dowels, 1 foot (30 cm) in length

1. Draw and cut out a pattern of a fish shape and trace two copies of it onto butcher paper or grocery bags.

2. Add realistic details like fins and scales.

3. Cut out the two shapes and staple them together around the edges, leaving the tail ends open. (See illustration below.)

4. Stuff the fish with loosely crumpled scrap paper.

5. Staple the tail closed.

6. Paint the fish with realistic colors.

7. Punch a hole in the fish's mouth and add colorful yarn for hanging.

8. Attach to a wooden dowel for waving the flag in your parade.

Fish Mobiles

Mobiles will remind you of fish swimming in schools, as they frequently do in the sea.

Materials

- fish patterns
- tagboard or light cardboard
- scissors
- tempera paint and paintbrushes, markers, or construction paper
- hole punch

- thread or light string, cut into lengths from 8 inches (3 cm) to 20 inches (8 cm)
- lightweight balsa wood pieces, 24 inches (9.5 cm) long
- lightweight sticks; 8 inch (3 cm) bamboo skewers are good
- lots of patience

1. Cut out 10–12 fish of different shapes. Decorate with paint, markers, or construction paper on one or both sides. (You may wish to add various fish facts to the backsides of the fish.)

2. Punch a hole at the top of each fish. (First hold the fish lightly between your fingers to find the best place to locate the hole so the fish will balance.) Tie a string through the hole.

3. Cross two long, sturdy sticks (balsa wood, thin dowels, or straight, thin tree branches) and temporarily secure at the cross point with string.

4. Attach another string at the point where the sticks cross to suspend the sticks from a ceiling girder, beam, or other high (and secure) location. Check the balance of the sticks, and adjust the positioning if needed. Secure well.

5. Tie two of the cutout fish on the ends of one stick. Tie the fish with different lengths of string. Check balance after adding the fish at the opposite ends of the stick.

6. Tie two bamboo skewers (with varying lengths of string) to the ends of the other stick. Center the skewers. Check for balance.

7. Loosely tie on two fish (using different lengths of string) to the ends of each of the bamboo skewers. Check for easy movement and balance; adjust, then tie securely.

8. Tie additional fish at the center of the mobile. Use varying lengths of string to allow free movement of all fish. Check for balance and adjust.

9. Add additional fish as desired. Be as elaborate and creative as you can. Display the mobile from a high location in your Caribbean display corner. If you have one, a spot that gets a gentle breeze is a nice place for this mobile.

Optional: Encourage children interested in birds to research different Caribbean species to make bird mobiles or bird flags (see p. 87 for flag directions).

Papier-mâché Butterflies

Materials

- tagboard
- butterfly patterns
- scissors, preferably sharp shears
- newspaper or newsprint
- flour paste
- wire

- paper towels
- tempera paint, paintbrushes
- felt-tip markers
- glitter
- sequins
- nail polish

1. Draw butterfly patterns on tagboard or enlarge and photocopy the examples shown here to create patterns. Cut out the patterns.

2. Prepare layers of pasted paper, with the top and bottom layers being plain paper towels (no printing).

3. Using the precut patterns, outline butterfly designs on the damp pasted layers of paper.

4. Cut out and mold in positions you choose (be extravagant!). Allow to dry.

5. Paint and decorate lavishly.

Bamboo

Bamboo is a grass that can be found in most tropical lands. It grows as much as 8 inches (20 cm) a day and can be found mainly in damp wooded areas such as in the Virgin Islands.

Bamboo stems are hollow and green in color when in the soil, but after the plant is cut, the leaves quickly wither and the stem becomes a golden color. There are many species of bamboo; however, the most common species found in the Caribbean area grows in clusters of plants as tall as 50 feet (16.5 m). Because of its strength and flexibility, many uses have been found for bamboo. A unique feature that helps give bamboo an appearance different from other plants is a dense crosspiece between the vertical lengths of the stem.

Bamboo Cups

By cutting a section of a very large piece of bamboo above one of the dense cross members, a cup can easily be fashioned and is actually used for beverages.

Bamboo Mats

Find straight bamboo that is approximately the diameter of a pencil and cut it into 12 inch (30 cm) pieces. Put the pieces next to each other, then bind the pieces near the top and bottom with raffia to make a usable and attractive place mat for table use.

Bamboo Chimes

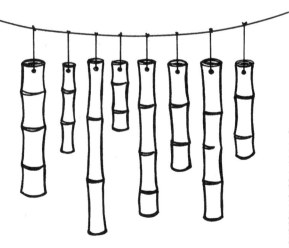

Locate bamboo that is approximately an inch in diameter and 6 inches (15 cm) to 15 inches (38 cm) long. (If necessary, cut long pieces into a variety of shorter lengths.) Drill or pierce holes in one end of the bamboo pieces. Suspend the bamboo loosely from strings tied to a 5-inch (12.5-cm) diameter ring or to a longer length of string stretched between two secure objects. The bamboo pieces will make a pleasant musical tone as they bump into each other in the wind or when gently tapped. In order for the pieces to vibrate, they must touch only their own string.

Shell Crafts

Many craft stores carry supplies like large bags of seashells and thick, water-resistant glue. To create various shell crafts, a silicone adhesive with "body" that can support the shells is best.

Group the shells by size, color, or shape. Grouping like shells makes design work a cinch. Make designs for:

wall plaques

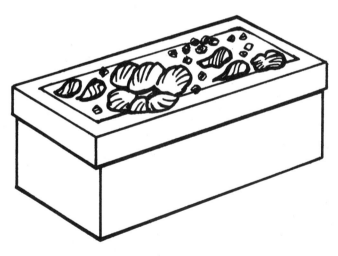

trinket boxes

glass jars

If you are too far from the ocean and real shells are difficult to obtain locally, try mail-order sources or use shell macaroni. Although macaroni is a last resort, it is inexpensive and a great creative opportunity.

Papier-mâché Fruit

Research fruits grown on Caribbean islands, then make several to add to the classroom display.

Materials

- armatures (Shapes to build sculptures around. For example, an armature could be a crumpled ball of newspaper held in place with masking tape, an inflated balloon, or an old ball.)

- flour paste

- narrow strips of newsprint

- plain paper towels or tissues

- tempera paint

- brushes

- shellac

1. On the chosen armature, paste strips of newsprint.

2. Build the fruit shape you are making with at least three layers of strips. Use narrower strips for smaller curves.

3. Use paper towels or tissues for the last paper layer.

4. Paint when the object has dried thoroughly.

5. Shellac.

For other pictures of Caribbean fruits, see pages 99–100 (Spin de Fruit game).

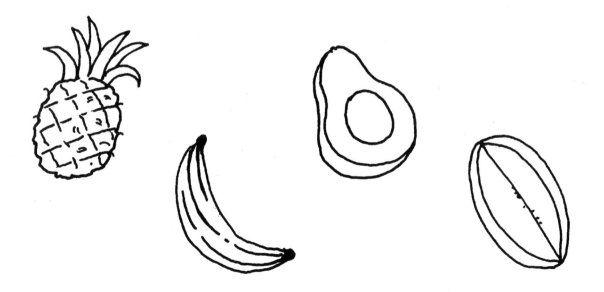

Tadjah

Materials

- boxes of graduated sizes
- shears
- wire
- strong tape
- paper-towel tubes
- flour paste and paper strips
- small balloons
- glue
- construction paper in bright colors or tempera paint and brushes
- markers
- glittery things (fabric, plastic, metal: sequins, metallic confetti)

1. Decide on a decorative building design for the tadjah. (See p. 31 for a tadjah example.)

2. Create a base for the tadjah by carefully cutting out a large piece of heavyweight cardboard.

3. Form the building structure by wiring together cardboard boxes of different sizes and shapes. (See diagram A below.) Strong tape can also fasten the boxes if desired.

4. Create decorative columns by building up paper-towel tubing with papier-mâché.

5. Add spires to the columns: Blow up several small balloons. Cover balloons with papier-mâché. Add extra strips at the tops to form spire points. (See diagram B.) Build in swirl shapes if desired. Let dry.

6. Glue or tape spires to top of columns and other box structures. Affix column bases to cardboard base.

7. Add lavish color with paint or colorful construction paper. Draw in elaborate designs with markers, then glue on glittery things to add to the ornateness.

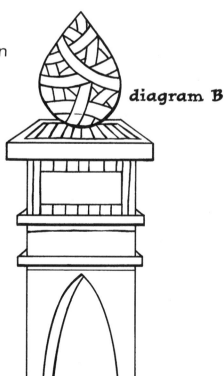

diagram B

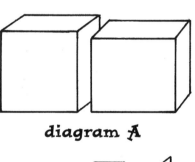

diagram A

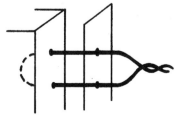

Baker's Clay

Materials

- 2 cups (200 g) flour
- 3/4 cup (180 ml) water
- 1/2 cup (100 g) salt
- food coloring (if desired)

Mix all ingredients and knead until smooth. Store dough at room temperature for two to three days or until dough hardens. (Dough will harden sooner if placed in a warm oven.)

Batik—Trinidad

Batik is a craft that has been perfected in the Caribbean. It is believed to have come from Indonesia and was developed there some 2,500 years ago.

In Batik, designs are sketched onto fabric with hot beeswax and paraffin. The most easy-to-use tool for this is a Japanese tjanting tool. The technique in batiking is known as wax-resist which means that a wax pattern applied to fabric resists the color of dyes when they are applied to the cloth. Early artisans who developed the technique used patterns that were exclusive to a family. These patterns were handed down from generation to generation for a thousand years.

Materials

- hot plate and asbestos pad
- foil
- small- to medium-size old glass or enamel saucepan
- paraffin and beeswax or crayons
- candy thermometer
- baking soda or salt
- cotton sheeting
- frame (canvas stretchers or an old picture frame) and tacks
- Japanese tjanting tool
- fabric dye
- rubber gloves
- plastic bucket
- paper towels
- iron
- newspaper
- brushes, 2-inches (10-cm) wide or smaller brushes, such as Japanese calligraphy brushes, which are inexpensive

1. Place the hot plate on an asbestos pad and foil. Using the saucepan, heat the wax to a temperature between 150°F (65°C) and 200°F (93°C). There is little danger of an accident if open flame is not used. Have a box of baking soda or salt nearby.

2. Stretch a piece of sheeting on a frame and tack in place. Apply a combination of melted paraffin and beeswax in lines on the stretched fabric. A simple design might be to dip the rim of a small cardboard jewelry box or paper cup in the hot wax and touch it to the cloth.

3. Mix the fabric dye in the plastic bucket and place the fabric in the dye. The longer you leave the piece in the dye, the darker the color will be. The dye will not color the parts of the fabric that have wax on them.

4. After the dye process, allow the fabric to dry and remove the wax by placing paper towels on both sides of the fabric and ironing on top of the paper towel. This should be done on thick pads of newspaper, which may also absorb some of the wax as it melts.

For a more involved batiking project (see below), use fine natural fabrics like those used in the Caribbean (sea-island cotton), or regular cotton, light wool, or inexpensive silk. It is best not to use synthetic fabrics because they do not take strong dyes.

1. Using the tjanting tool, make detailed wax designs, then dye the fabric.

2. Remove the wax by placing an iron on paper towels. If using more than one color or for detailed work, cleaning fluid will dissolve wax completely. Protect with wax any spaces on the design that you wish to preserve before applying another color.

3. If you wish to show a crackled effect in the dying, use more paraffin than beeswax. Generally the mixture is 60% beeswax and 40% paraffin. To get a crackly effect, increase the paraffin to 60% or 70%. While dyeing the material, leave the material in the dye until the desired depth of color is achieved, then rinse in clear water. Bleach will remove stains from a sink.

Box Theater

Use this special "movie" theater to present a story about one of the Caribbean island's festivals, crops, or other subject of interest.

Materials

- cardboard shoeboxes
- sharp shears or scissors
- strips of nonstick shelf paper
- pencils, pens, or markers
- crayons or paint and brushes for illustrating the story
- two 1-inch (2.5-cm) dowels
- thumbtacks or tape

1. Cut one of the long ends out of a shoebox.

2. Cut another, smaller opening in the other long end.

3. Write your story, comic-strip style, on one side of a long sheet of shelf paper. Add illustrations with paint or crayons.

4. Cut holes 1 inch (2.5 cm) in diameter in the top of the shoebox. Make sure the dowels fit snugly into the holes. The distance between the holes should be the same as the length of the section cut in Step 1.

5. Cut matching holes through the bottom of the shoebox.

6. Tack or tape one end of the decorated shelf paper to one dowel and the other end to the second dowel, parchment or scroll style.

7. Remove the shoebox top, insert the bottoms of the dowels into the two bottom holes, then replace the box top, fitting the tops of the dowels into the holes.

8. Turn dowels (in the same direction) from the bottom to show your box-theater story.

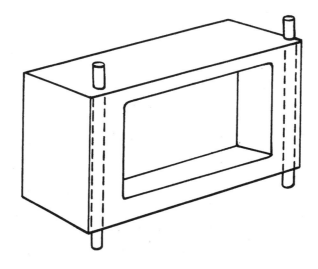

Cork Stork

Materials

- corks
- small tack hammer
- nail
- pipe cleaners
- construction paper
- glue
- colored feathers

1. Place cork on a work surface and, using the hammer, tap the nail in where you think legs and neck should be located.

2. Remove the nail and insert a pipe cleaner into the top hole for the neck, and two pipe cleaners into the bottom holes, for the legs.

3. Make interesting features for the head and bill out of construction paper. Glue these onto the pipe-cleaner neck. Twist extra pieces of pipe cleaner onto the bottoms of the legs to create feet.

4. Make a pipe cleaner tail or perhaps add a couple of small, colorful feathers for a tail and wings (they're easy to find).

Calypso Tent

Materials

- 6-foot (2-m) long 2-inch by 4-inch (5-cm by 10-cm) piece of wood; sturdy, straight stick; or mop or broom handle

- pail full of stones, gravel, or sand

- 5 gallon (20 l) pail

- 30–40 pounds (13.5–18 kg) plaster of Paris

- cloth or sheet, size of desired tent

- wire

- 2 long, straight sticks or two-by-twos

1. Fix the long piece of wood in a pail of stones, sand, or plaster of Paris.

2. Tack the cloth along the top of the chalkboards on two walls in a corner of the classroom. (See diagram below.)

3. Add a decorative edge to the front of the tent and if you are ambitious, also along the chalkboard tops.

4. Wire point *A* to the stick in the pail.

5. Furniture could be nail kegs or overturned plastic buckets.

6. Lightweight sticks (or extra two by twos) would be nice supports for the front edges of the tent top (*B* and *C*).

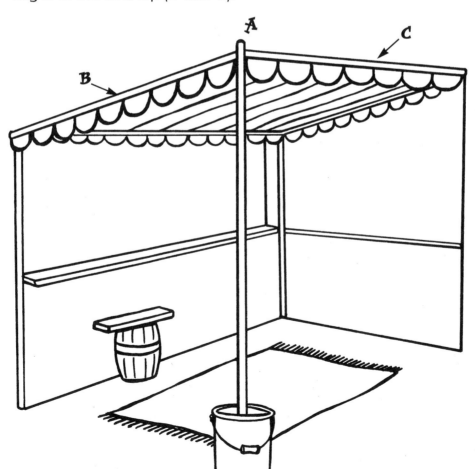

Spin de Fruit—Haiti

For this Carnival game, pictures of fruit can be used if real samples are not available.

Materials

- 2 large pieces of posterboard
- scissors
- markers

- copies of Caribbean fruits pictured below, enlarged if desired
- brass fastener

1. Draw and cut out a large circle from one piece of posterboard. Cut a similar-size square from the other piece.

2. Mark off about 12 sections of the circle where fruit will be positioned. You may want to demarcate each section using a different color.

3. Enlarge, photocopy, and cut out the pictures of the fruits below and on page 100, or draw and cut out fruit shapes. Color as indicated.

4. Make a hole in the center of your fruit circle and in the center of the other piece of posterboard.

5. Push the fastener through the fruit circle and the posterboard square. Fasten just tightly enough so that circle will be able to spin.

6. Draw an arrow in one corner of the square pointing toward the fruit circle.

star fruit (or carambola)
light green

soursop
light green

cherimoya
light green

breadfruit
light green

pineapple
tan and green

guava
light yellow-green

pawpaw (or papaya)
rosy or golden

banana
yellow

avocado
dark green

lemon
yellow

mango
pink and yellow

passion fruit
yellow, purple, or brown

Wiss Vine Basket—Virgin Islands

The wiss vine, or basket wiss, is a plant that grows in the Virgin Islands. It is a woody slender vine that clings to trees and shrubs. Because it is not readily available, try working with reed, a material found in craft shops or school-supply stores and used for weaving baskets.

Soak the reed before using it because it can be very brittle and easily broken when dry. It's also possible to dye reed with hot water dye for variety in design. This should be done before any weaving is done. (See p. 112 to make plant dyes.)

Materials

- food or plant dye (if desired)
- reed

- bucket of water
- scissors or side-cutting nippers

1. Start with two sets of four long reeds crossed at their centers. Bind the center securely with another piece of reed. (See diagram below.) Secure the end of the binder reed under one of the cross members.

2. Use a long, well-soaked reed as a threader and begin weaving it under and over the reeds that are bound together, such as *under A, over B, under C, over D, under 1, over 2,* and so on.

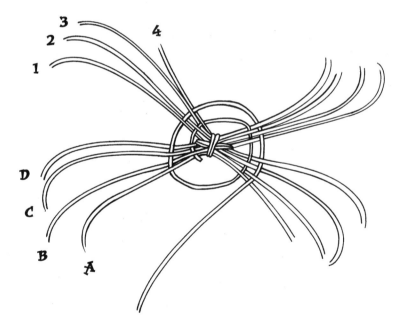

3. As you work, you may need to wet the reeds several times. If so, dip the whole project in a bucket of water.

4. Keep weaving, spreading the spokes of the basket apart evenly. The further from the center that you get, the easier it will be to spread the spokes apart.

5. Eventually (about six times around), one lone spoke can be added to make an odd number of spines to the basket.

Calabash Objects

It is possible to make objects from the calabash (gourds), however a facsimile is probably necessary because it can be difficult to find if you are not in the Caribbean islands. If you are lucky enough to work with the real thing, a calabash must have been picked as many as nine months beforehand so that it is completely dry. When dry, it is extremely light. (While growing, it was mostly water.) The hard shell is remarkably tough and must be cut with a hacksaw.

Papier-mâché spheres work as well if they are thoroughly dried before you try to cut into them. Use at least seven to ten layers of paper to create a strong form with which to work. To provide the best surface for painting, make the final layer of paper from plain paper towels. Again, it is suggested that the cutting be done with a hacksaw.

Materials

- sphere-shaped calabash or papier-mâché sphere

- hacksaw

- sandpaper

1. Using the hacksaw, carefully cut the dry calabash or sphere in two. (Note: You may wish to do this for your students ahead of time.)

2. Remove the fibers and other loose materials that remain on the inside of the calabash halves.

3. Use sandpaper to smooth the rims of the calabashes and to clean the inner surfaces.

Calabash Bowls

Calabash Footed Bowl

For a footed bowl, glue a small calabash half to the bottom of a larger calabash half.

Calabash Maracas

Make a hole in each sphere exactly the size of the dowel's diameter. Add a few dried beans, dried corn kernels, or pebbles for the "noisemakers" and glue the handle firmly in place. The surface may be easily decorated with felt-tip markers or acrylic or oil paints. To get a high gloss, add two coats of shellac.

Calabash Lantern

If the object is large enough, it could be used for a decorative hanging lamp. Bore small holes in the sphere to let light shine through. Bore a larger hole to fit an electric light bulb assembly (available at hardware and home building-supply stores). Glue the light assembly in place and let dry. Attach a lightweight cord to the top of the lantern and hang in your display corner.

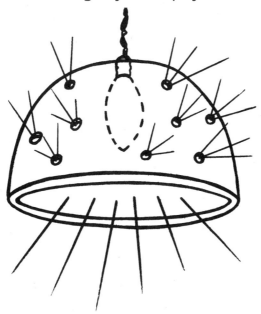

Seed Art

Seeds provide food and start life. They can also be used for decoration. There are countless ways that seeds can be fashioned into things of beauty, especially for adornment, mostly because of their symbolic meaning as the origin of life.

Seed Paintings

Seeds come in a great variety of colors and can be used to create seed paintings with seeds arranged in interesting ways on a hard surface. All plants have flowers and develop some sort of seed. Many are small and hard to find; others are larger and more plentiful. Collect and dry small seeds and seed parts, such as the following, to use to create your seed paintings.

acorn caps	buckwheat	kidney beans	peas	sunflower
allspice	cantaloupe	lima beans	poppy	watermelon
apple	corn	navy beans	pumpkin	wheat
beans	grass	oats	squash	

Materials

- sturdy cardboard, masonite, or thin plywood
- pencil
- variety of seeds
- white glue

1. On stiff cardboard or a piece of masonite or thin plywood, create a drawing that does not have a great deal of detail.

2. Decide which seeds you will use to cover each section of your drawing.

3. Paint with white glue an area that should be covered with a particular type or color of seed and then sprinkle those seeds on the glued area.

4. Let stand for a few minutes and then pour off the excess seeds, saving them to use another time. Do not be in too great a rush, and be very patient in waiting for the glue to dry before adding new seeds.

5. Continue this process to complete the painting, allowing time between applications of different seeds.

Seed Jewelry

Seeds large enough to have holes put through them will make fascinating jewelry. After the seeds are drilled or pierced, patterns can be made with the different-shaped seeds. An awl or sewing needle can be used to pierce seeds that are not too old or those that have been soaked ahead of time. Sometimes harder seeds will need to be drilled beforehand with an electric drill. Seeds as small as watermelon seeds are great for an art piece such as a necklace, anklet, or bracelet. Seeds may be interspersed with glass or plastic beads to make interesting patterns. Thread seeds on dental floss, and when stringing is done, make shiny with shellac.

Seed Necklaces

Materials

- dried seeds (sunflower, allspice, cantaloupe, squash, coffee beans, apple, pumpkin, watermelon, acorns, acorn caps, beans)

- large needles

- dental floss or carpet thread

1. Soak hard seeds before trying to pierce the seeds with a needle.

2. Decide on a design pattern (such as one small seed, one medium seed, one large seed; or one small, two large, one small, and two medium seeds) before starting and be consistent.

3. Thread seeds on carpet thread or dental floss. Place hard seeds on a flat surface and push the needle through the seed, so that the point goes onto a protected table or hard surface rather than into a finger.

Mr. Harding (Oversized Effigy)

Materials

- 2-inch by 4-inch (5-cm by 10-cm) piece of wood, 6 feet (2 m) long (for armature)

- 12 inch by 12 inch (30 cm x 30 cm) 1-inch (2.5-cm) thick piece of plywood or heavy wooden board (for base)

- nails

- hammer

- chicken wire

- papier-mâché paste, large paper strips and sheets

- tempera paint and paintbrushes

1. Nail the two-by-four onto the wooden base to create an armature. Put the chicken wire around the wood armature, shaping it to look roughly like a human figure.

2. Cover the chicken wire with papier-mâché. Since Mr. Harding is big, use large sheets of paper to cover the wire quickly.

3. Add details as desired. Paint after figure dries.

at least 6 feet

Crop Over Carts

Materials

- large matchbox
- construction paper
- scissors
- glue or paste
- small paper or plastic flowers
- tagboard
- tongue depressor
- markers
- toy people or miniature Crop Over materials

1. Glue construction paper on the match box to cover the outside and inside of the box.
2. Glue the flowers onto the matchbox to decorate.
3. Cut wheels out of tagboard and glue these onto the matchbox.
4. A tongue depressor for the wagon handle can be glued to the front center of the box.
5. A decorative panel can be affixed at the back of the wagon. (See p. 64.)
6. Load the wagon with toy people or Crop Over materials.

Gold Bracelet

Materials

- tape measure
- tagboard or wire
- scissors
- newspaper strips
- papier-mâché paste
- gold spray paint
- plastic gemstones
- spray shellac

1. Close one hand into a fist and measure the widest part of the fist.
2. Cut a strip of tagboard or wire slightly longer than the fist measurement.
3. Diagonally wrap several layers of pasted newspaper strips around the tagboard strip or wire.
4. While it is still pliable, join the ends of the wire or tagboard strip to make a bracelet.
5. Allow to dry for a couple of days.
6. Use additional papier-mâché mash to increase the thickness of the bracelet.
7. When the desired shape is achieved and the bracelet is completely dry, spray on the gold paint. After the paint has dried, glue on the plastic gemstones.

Optional: Before "gemstones" are glued onto the bracelet, make the gold shine more by applying two coats of shellac. (See illustration on p. 40.)

Printmaking

Printmaking is transferring ink or paint from one surface to another.

Materials

- tagboard
- pencil
- scissors
- glue
- brayer or brushes
- tempera paint (wet) or ink
- paper

1. Draw on tagboard a design with a Caribbean theme, such as a fish, fruit, or bird.
2. Cut out the design and glue it onto another piece of tagboard.
3. Add a few details with smaller pieces of tagboard.
4. Use brayer or brush and paint the design.
5. When the design is charged with paint, lay a piece of paper on the painted surface, press down firmly, and lift off carefully.

Several copies can be made before the tagboard becomes too soft.

Print From 3-D Object

It is possible to paint directly onto a physical object such as a plastic fish or shell and then get a print by placing a clean paper on the object.

Materials

- 3-D object for printing, such as a small fish, feather, or shell
- newspaper
- paintbrushes
- tempera paint
- paper

1. Lay the object on newspaper and apply tempera paint.
2. Lay a piece of plain paper over the painted object, and gently press the paper with your hand.
3. Remove the paper. The print of the object will be made on the underside of the paper.

Uniprint (one print)

There are so many ways to do printing; this is a rather magical one to try.

Materials

- paper
- Japanese brayer
- paint or printing ink
- pencil

1. Place a piece of paper on a flat surface such as a tabletop or piece of plate acrylic.

2. Use a brayer to place a charge of ink or paint on the paper.

3. Very carefully, place a sheet of clean paper on the freshly painted paper and draw a design with pencil on the top paper. Where you make a pencil mark, ink or paint will be pulled onto the underside of the paper.

4. Lift the top paper off carefully and let dry.

Potato Prints

Materials

- potatoes
- sharp knives or utility knives
- ink or tempera paint
- paper
- markers (optional)

1. Cut a potato in half to create two flat surfaces.

2. Think of a repeated design pattern. Carefully cut pieces of the potato away, leaving behind a simple raised design such as a triangle or a square.

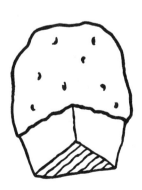  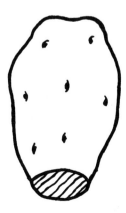

3. Brush paint on the raised design surface of the potato.

4. Touch the raised surface to the paper to leave a design print.

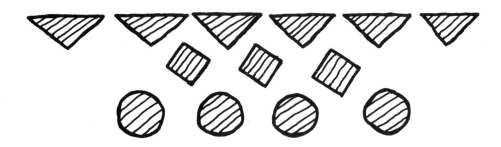

5. Continue adding potato prints to create the chosen pattern.

A trick to emphasize a design more is to use a marker to add a line around the printed design after the paint is dry.

Printing With Art Gum

The pottery designs shown on page 111 were found in ancient Antigua and are good examples to use in making your own art-gum prints. Art-gum erasers will crumble easily and can disintegrate quickly; however, if handled carefully, the erasers will print well and last a long time.

Materials

- art paper and pencil

- art-gum erasers

- pencil or pointed instrument such as a worn-out ballpoint pen

- ink or paint

- object to be imprinted, such as heavy paper or pottery

1. Plan your design by drawing the design on art paper.

2. Transfer the simple line design to the art gum eraser.

3. Gently and carefully trace over the lines a number of times to wear grooves into the eraser. This will create the design stamp.

4. Cover the designed surface of the stamp with ink or paint and stamp it where you want it to print. The design will appear as long as ink or paint is not applied too heavily.

5. Change colors if desired for different parts of your design.

Art Gum Designs

Dyeing With Plant Dye

Materials

- water
- enamel pot
- stove or single burner
- red-onion skins (for reddish purple dye) or yellow-onion skins (for a brownish yellow dye)

- wooden spoon
- strainer
- copper pennies or iron frying pan (optional)

1. Heat a half gallon (2 l) of water in an enamel pot. Add six or seven handfuls of red- or yellow-onion skins and simmer for an hour.

2. Strain the solution and discard the skins.

3. To intensify the dye, boil away much of the water until the dye is darker. For a brighter color, add copper pennies to the dye in the enamel pot. To make the color darker, put the dye in an iron frying pan and continue heating until the desired shade is obtained.

Designs in Steel—Haiti

Unrest and extreme poverty did not allow for much artistic development over the centuries in Haiti. In 1944, when the Centre d'Art opened, it was found that many people had been working privately. Much had been created on flat pieces of black metal using intricate but simple designs showing common things, such as flowers, animals, and plants. The silhouettes were then cut out. To simulate these steel designs, use heavy paper, tagboard, or cardboard to create cutout designs and spray them with flat black paint, or use the directions following and on page 114.

Materials

- construction paper, tagboard, or light cardboard

- markers

- light-colored crayons

- pencils

- heavy layers of newspapers or thick cardboard

- utility knives (for children old enough to use them) or scissors

1. Draw designs on construction paper, using subjects from nature.

2. Use markers to darken the outlines. Designs can also be drawn on art paper.

3. Cover the back of the design with light-colored crayon applied heavily.

4. Transfer the design by placing the paper, face up, on black paper and tracing the design, bearing down hard to transfer the crayon.

5. Place the completed transfer on a thick stack of newspaper (to protect the table) and carefully cut out the design with a utility knife. Or use scissors.

Coat of Arms

Create a personal or class coat of arms, like those of Jamaica (below), or Puerto Rico (see p. 70).

Materials

- drawing and construction paper
- crayons or markers
- pencils
- laminating plastic (optional)

1. Select features to be included in the coat of arms by asking questions such as *What are the class's favorite subjects, activities, seasons of the year, or foods? How many boys and girls are in the class? What is the geography of the town or city where you live? Is your area usually cold and snowy, hot and dry, balmy and green with lots of plant growth?* If making an individual crest, ask these questions: *How many sisters and brothers do you have? Did your family immigrate to the United States from another country? If so, from where? What kind of home do you live in—a house, condominium, apartment, mobile home? What family pets do you have?*

2. Create designs for the features selected.

3. Draw final designs on construction paper and color to create your own coat of arms. You may wish to laminate the finished crest(s) and display in the classroom.

Mango Seed Dolls

Materials

- mango seed
- markers
- cloth scraps

- scissors
- glue
- scrap paper

1. Eat a ripe mango and save the large flat seed, including the fibers that run along the edges of the seed.

2. Dry the seed.

3. Use markers to draw a face on the seed.

4. Glue on scraps of cloth to make clothes for the doll. Stuff the clothes with paper or make into a hand puppet.

Clay Coil Pots

An extremely useful craft to know how to make is the coil pot. (See example on p. 44.) Coil pots can be used as containers or for making the tassa drums (p. 176) and deya lamps (p. 117) used in the Hindu Divali festival. Be sure to use low-fire clay, which can be obtained at a school-supply store.

Materials

- low-fire clay
- smoothing sticks (helpful, but fingers work just as well)

- water
- kiln

1. Make long ropelike pieces of clay and coil them around so that the sides of the coil are fixed tight together. The more quickly you work the better, for if the clay dries out, it will not stick well.

2. Where the edges of the coil touch, scratch the wet clay with your fingernail and apply a bit of "slip" (a creamy mixture of water and clay) before pushing the coils together.

3. After the coils are joined, smooth out the ridges of the coils with your fingers to make a more even surface for the container, particularly on the inside surface.

4. It will probably take at least a week before the containers can be put in the kiln. If they contain too much moisture they will explode. Dry the pots slowly away from drafts, and be sure to fire the pieces *extremely slowly*. Follow the directions on the package of the clay with which you are working and fire at the prescribed temperature.

Deya Lamps—Trinidad and Tobago

The Hindu religion was introduced to Trinidad in 1845. The Hindu custom of lighting a series of deya lamps is part of the Divali celebration. Deya lamps (small earthenware lamps or coil pots filled with oil with a wick added) are arranged in a cluster or row of lights. (*Divali* means "row of lights.") These coil pots are set on bamboo stands and lighted. A string of lights may also be woven through tree branches.

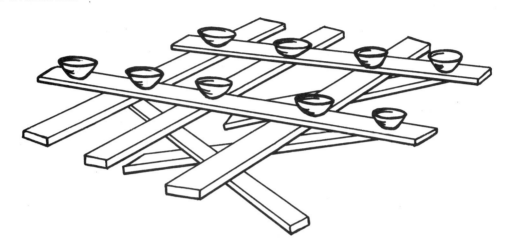

Wattle Wall Panel

Small temporary huts are usually constructed from materials that grow in the islands. A wattle wall is made by taking inch-thick saplings and standing them vertically in cement for support. When the cement has hardened, thinner branches (or softened reed) are woven through the sapling pieces.

To make a facsimile of such a panel, instead of cement, use plaster of Paris, which sets up quickly.

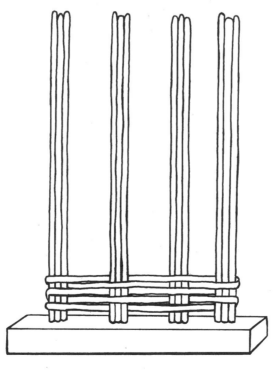

Tying Knots

Encourage children who enjoy knot tying to research how each of the knots below are used. Children may also enjoy searching the library for books and other resources on macramé.

Materials

- light cotton or synthetic rope, or macramé cord

Using 6- to 12-inch (30- to 60-cm) lengths of rope or cord, carefully follow the pictures shown below to make each of the knots.

square knot or reef knot

carrick bend

sheepshank

bowline

clove hitch

diagram A

diagram B

diagram C

Matchbox Boat

Materials

- empty matchboxes or half-pint milk cartons cut down to 1 inch (2.5 cm) from bottoms
- construction paper
- scissors
- glue
- lollipop sticks or coffee stirrers
- modeling clay (optional)

1. Using the matchbox base or cut-down milk carton, cover the sides and bottom with construction paper to form the boat's hull. Add a triangular section at one end of the hull to create the boat's bow.

2. Glue a lollipop stick or coffee stirrer to the matchbox or stand it in a small lump of modeling clay to make the mast.

3. Draw and cut out sails and a flag from construction paper. Glue these to the mast.

If several boats are built, a boat race could be held. Float the boats in a water tray or dishpan filled partway with water. Use a small electric fan to create a light breeze to send the boats sailing.

Cartography

Maps are needed if you are going to the Caribbean. There are thousands of Caribbean islands—some tiny, some very large. Without a map it would be all too easy to get lost trying to find your way! A realistic map of several Caribbean islands or a make-believe map for treasure hunters can be created by following the steps below.

Materials

- pencils, pens
- sturdy paper
- colored pencils
- markers or crayons
- water
- watercolors

1. Decide on the design of your map by selecting the Caribbean islands you would like to include or by creating an imaginary location. Draw your map. Then locate your buried treasure. Add features such as cities, towns, rivers, lakes, mountains, swamps, deserts, forests, trees, direction signs, pathways, and so on, as appropriate.

2. Think of how you would like the water to be shown at the shoreline. Choose one style of water detail and add this around the island or islands. (See diagram on p. 120 for an example.)

3. Use different colors to show the land and water areas.

4. Place a compass rose in one corner of the map.

5. Add a label to your map.

6. To make the map look old, distress the paper by gently tearing the edges or by wetting the paper and applying brown watercolor paint to the edges.

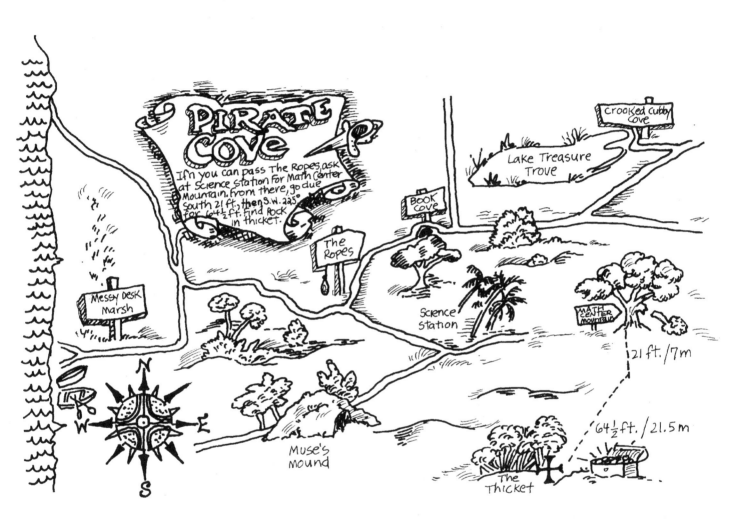

Walnut-Shell Turtles

Materials

- unbroken walnut-shell halves
- construction paper
- scissors
- markers
- glue

1. Place the empty walnut shell on a work surface, with the opening face down.

2. From construction paper, design and cut out four feet, a head, and a tail. Glue these in place on the walnut shell.

Walnut-Shell Whales

Materials

- unbroken walnut-shell halves
- construction paper
- scissors
- markers
- glue

1. Position the walnut shell on a work surface, with the opening face down.

2. Design eyes, a tail, and fins with pieces of construction paper, then glue these in place on the walnut shell.

Tote Bag With Caribbean Designs

A practical gift that children could make is a decorated tote bag. Many craft stores have inexpensive, lightweight canvas totes that can be painted. Sometimes parents are willing to help by making simple bags out of appropriate fabric.

Materials

- paper and pencil

- commercial or homemade tote bag, or 12- by 15-inch (4.7- by 6-cm) piece of fabric for making the front side of a tote

- permanent fabric markers in a variety of bright colors

- thick fabric paint, such as puff paint or glossy paint that can be found in craft stores (optional)

1. Draw a design of Caribbean fruits, birds, fish, plants, or other items on a piece of paper.

2. Transfer the finished design to the tote bag, using permanent fabric markers in a variety of colors, or mark the design in the middle of a piece of fabric if the bag is to be assembled later.

3. If desired, use fabric paint to outline the objects on the tote bag.

Kites

Materials

- two half-inch-thick sticks, 2 feet (60 cm) and 3 feet (1 m) in length
- utility knife
- string
- sturdy paper or cloth, about 1 yard (1 m) long
- glue
- cloth scraps (for tail)
- paint and brushes

1. Carve notches in the tips of the two sticks to hold the string in place. Cross the sticks and fasten the intersection securely.

2. Stretch a length of string tightly from one side to the other to put a slight bend in the shorter kite stick. Fasten the string at each end.

3. Wrap a long length of string all the way around this kite frame, placing string in the grooved tips of both sticks. Fasten tightly at the tip of one stick.

4. Cut paper or cloth to overhang the stick frame by several inches on all sides.

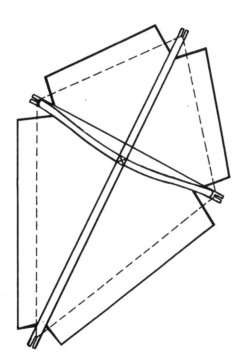

5. Wrap the edges of the paper or cloth around the outer string. Fold over and glue in place. Let dry.

6. Add a tail to the end of the kite and tie on strips of cloth for balance—the stronger the wind, the steadier the kite will fly with a weighted tail.

7. Paint pictures of animals, such as frogs or birds, on the front of the kite, if desired.

Holiday Ornaments—Puerto Rico

To be authentic, use natural materials if possible. To make holiday ornaments, search for calabashes or gourds that are nearly round in shape. Sometimes in the fall you can find small gourds in grocery stores. Allow them to dry out completely. When dry, they become extremely hard and can be a bit moldy looking; however, this does not affect their suitability for ornament-making.

Materials

- calabashes or gourds
- sandpaper
- spray paint (use outdoors)
- screw eyes
- glue
- glitter
- sequins
- acrylic paint, brushes
- paint pens
- mirrors, feathers, bones, seeds, leaves (optional)
- ribbon, papier-mâché

1. Using heavy sandpaper, remove any bumps or blemishes from the gourd. Then spray-paint the gourd. (The smoother the surface, the easier it will be to add painted details later on.)

2. At the narrow end, insert a screw eye from which to hang the finished piece.

3. Glue on sequins, glitter, or buttons, making a bright colorful design.

4. Use acrylic paint or paint pens to add detail.

5. Mirrors, feathers, bones, or any other materials found in the Caribbean can also be included.

Since the calabash may be difficult to find, plastic foam balls (available in craft stores) can be used instead. Use pins to cover the balls with ribbons. Papier-mâché can also be easily put around the plastic foam to create a sturdy surface for decorating with paint and sparkly objects.

Paper-Bag Masks

Materials

- brown grocery bags (20-pound weight)
- scissors
- construction paper
- paste or glue
- felt-tip markers
- sequins
- feathers

1. Cut the sides of the bag so that the top of the wearer's head hits the inside bottom of the bag.

2. Cut out eye and mouth holes after locating and marking them.

3. To add features, paste or glue pieces of construction paper to the paper bag and decorate with markers, sequins, and feathers.

Papier-mâché Masks

Materials

- newsprint paper or balloon
- papier-mâché and newspaper strips
- scissors
- tempera paint and brushes
- shellac (optional)
- string, shoelaces, or elastic ties

1. Crumple a sheet of newsprint paper to form an armature (the form that will support the papier-mâché strips) or use a balloon.

2. Paste several layers of newsprint over one half of the armature to form a mask.

3. After the newsprint has been pasted in place, build up facial features such as the chin, lips, nose, and forehead. Narrow strips work best for sharper details. Create ears last.

4. When the mask is dry (allow at least two days), trim off the ends of the strips that were pasted to the original armature paper.

5. Pierce and trim holes for eyes. Add holes on the sides of the masks for strings, shoelaces, or elastic ties.

6. Paint masks with tempera. Let dry, then shellac.

7. Attach ties.

Paper-Bag Hand Puppet

Materials

- pencil and paper
- paper lunch bag
- construction paper
- scissors
- paste or glue
- markers

1. Plan a design for the hand puppet.

2. Place the paper bag upside down with the fold created by the bottom of the bag face up. Draw eyes, nose, forehead, and hair features above the fold. Draw the upper lip so that the edges meet the fold.

3. Below the fold, draw the lower lip so that the edges meet the fold. Then add the chin and neck. Draw the tongue under the flap of the bag.

4. Cut out pieces of construction paper and glue or paste in position to complete the design.

5. Add details with markers or crayons.

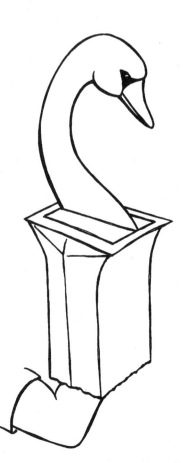

animal-head puppets

Carnival Costumes

Adorn at least the neck, wrists, and ankles of every Carnival participant. (See sample neck and wrist adornments below.) Shiny ankle ornaments help attract the attention of the parade audience.

Carnival Costumes

Jonkanoo Costumes—
Jamaica, the Bahamas

Jonkanoo costumes are unique in that they help portray some definite characters who enact the events of the Jonkanoo celebration. All of the costumes are somewhat crudely made and may look very quickly done. The characters frequently wear wire-screen masks. One of the "actors" dresses in what is known as pitchy-patchy. A second character represents a devil and the third, an animal. The animal head may be worn on top of the head as a hat. A wire-screen mask, with painted accent marks for a mouth, covers the face. Vision holes are fixed in the mask and are outlined with paint for emphasis.

 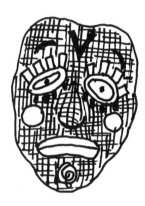  

Wire-Screen Masks

Materials

- masking tape
- wire screen
- newspaper
- tempera paints, paintbrushes
- shoelaces, twill tape, or string (for mask ties)

1. Affix masking tape around the edges of a piece of wire screen that is about the size of a person's face from ear to ear and hairline to Adam's apple.

2. Place the screen over the person's face and gently push or bend the wire to somewhat match the location of the nose and eyes and the general shape of the face. Don't worry if it looks a bit crude.

3. Put the screen on a newspaper-covered table and paint on spots, mouth, lines around the eyes, eyebrows, and any interesting designs you wish.

4. To wear, add ties to the sides and tie at the back of the head.

Pitchy Patchy

Materials

- old shirt and pants, or old dress

- scraps of bright-colored cloth,
  1 1/2 inches wide by 6 inches long (4 cm by 15 cm)

- stapler (or needle, thread, and scissors)

There is no definite pattern for this costume. Starting at the bottom, cover the old garment with layers of bright-colored cloth strips. Attach fabric strips vertically with either needle and thread or stapler, working from the center, or inside, of the garment out. Overlap rows of strips and tack on in any design or color order you like.

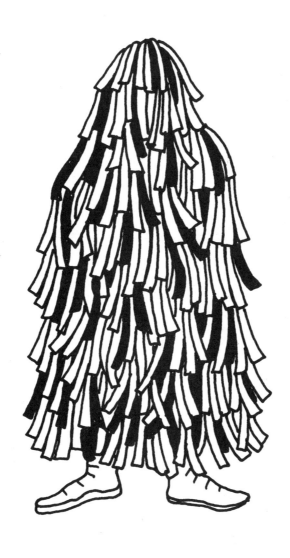

Devil and Bull Horns Hat

Materials

- old hat (a brimless hat or baseball cap works best)
- two cardboard paper-towel tubes
- scissors
- tape
- papier-mâché materials
- glue
- tempera paint and brushes

1. Make a set of animal horns with papier-mâché and the paper-towel tubes. Cut three long slits into the ends of the tubes.

2. Press the cut ends together to form the tips of the horns. Tape in place, then apply the papier mâché, building it up and bending each tube into the desired shape. Let dry.

3. Glue the horns to the hat. Add papier-mâché to the hat and horns to build up features as desired. Let dry thoroughly.

4. Paint the headpiece.

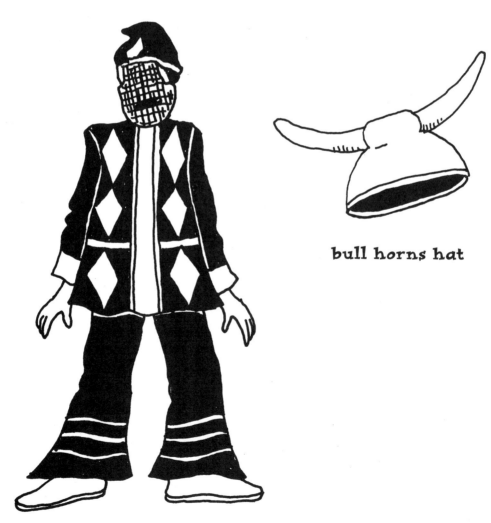

bull horns hat

devil

Animal Head

Materials

- old hat
- tempera paint and paintbrushes
- papier-mâché materials
- tape
- cardboard (optional)
- fabric pieces, 2 yards (2 m)
- glue

1. With the hat and papier-mâché, fashion the head of a real or imaginary animal. Cardboard may be used to help form larger animal heads. Usually these masks fit over the entire head, so try to include a front and back in your design.

2. Decorate with gaudy colors.

3. Attach pieces of cloth, flowing from the bottom of the mask like a mini-cape, to help seclude the actor.

Three Wild Indians

Horsehead

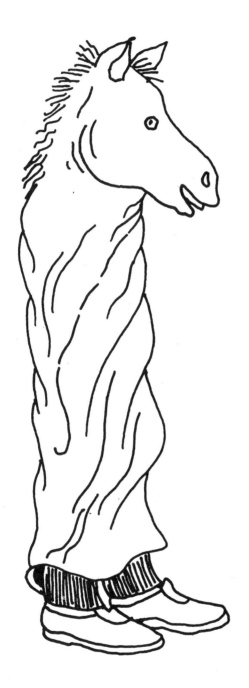

Fancy Crown

Man's Fancy Dress

Lady's Fancy Dress

Rara Costumes—Haiti

Rara costumes use flashy tinsel, mirrors, sequins, and bright-colored cloth. Multicolored scarves and strips of cloth are fastened to clothing. The jonc's tunic is in the shape of a serape or huge collarlike dickey that extends from the belt line in front to midback. The tunic is elaborately sequined and decorated. The queens wear fancy, floor-length, bright-colored dresses of taffeta or rayon; elaborate, jeweled headwraps or broad-brimmed hats decorated with various-colored cloth strips; gloves; baubles; and ruffled petticoats.

Rara Headpieces

Caribbean Foods

Ackee/akee ▪ A triangular hanging fruit from Jamaica. The center is soft, with the texture of scrambled eggs, and has a lemony taste. It is served with fish and vegetables.

Acrats/accras ▪ Nicknamed "Stamp and Go." This spicy hot fritter is sold at food stands throughout the Caribbean. (For a recipe, see page 153.)

Blaff ▪ A broth that contains whole Scotch bonnet peppers.

Breadfruit ▪ A large green fruit used as a vegetable. The whole fruit can be roasted in its skin for 45 minutes and eaten hot. (See picture on p. 100.)

Callaloo/callilu/calaloo/callalou ▪ The tender green leaves of the dasheen plant, similar to spinach or kale, used mainly for callaloo soup.

Cassava/gucca/manioc ▪ A root vegetable about the size and shape of a turnip. It has scaly skin and is used principally for making flour. Cassava is poisonous until cooked.

Cherimoya ▪ A pale green, bumpy fruit with sweet white flesh that has the texture of soft pudding. The fruit is eaten fully ripe and well chilled. (See picture on p. 99.)

Cho-cho ▪ A small pear-shaped green vegetable with prickly skin. Like the papaya, it is used as a meat tenderizer.

Coconut water ▪ Water from the green nut makes a delicious soft drink.

Dasheen/taro ▪ Edible root of the taro plant. It is peeled and boiled in salted water. Can also be fried, creamed, or roasted.

Guava/guayaba ▪ A rich, pear-shaped fruit that can be eaten raw or made into jelly. Its many small, hard seeds are used to sweeten drinks, jams, chutney, and syrups. (See picture on p. 100.)

Heart of palm ▪ The cream-colored center of the bud of cabbage palm trees.

Hibiscus ▪ A tropical flower (not the garden variety), grown for its bright red center and used to flavor drinks, jams, and sauces.

Mango ▪ A fruit of various sizes, shapes, and textures. It starts as a green bulb and usually turns pink with a strong odor and sweet taste. (See picture on p. 100.)

Okra/okroe/lady's fingers/gumbo ▪ This finger-shaped vegetable grows to about 4 inches (10 cm). It can be fried, used as a thickener in callaloo, or mixed with cornmeal to make Cornmeal Cou Cou (p. 152).

Pawpaw/papaya ▪ A sweet, rosy or golden fruit that, before it ripens, can be stuffed and baked. The ripened fruit is used in jams, sauces, juices, and as a dessert. Delicious by itself sprinkled with a little lime juice. (See picture on p. 100.)

Passion fruit ▪ Oval shaped, yellow, purple, or deep brown fruit with a tough shell. The meat is sweet but must be strained before it is used in desserts, juices, and sauces. (See picture on p. 100.)

Plantain ▪ A large bananalike fruit that is best eaten roasted, boiled, mashed, or fried. (See recipes on pp. 150 and 154.)

Seville orange ▪ A bittersweet fruit transplanted from Spain and used in making marmalade and marinades.

Soursop ▪ A spiked fruit shaped like an extra-large strawberry or a pine cone, it's both sour and sweet; used in drinks, sherbets, and ice cream. (See picture on p. 99 and punch recipe on p. 151.)

Sweetsop/sugar apple ▪ A member of the cherimoya family that is always served fresh.

Sugar cane ▪ Sugar cane comes from the same family as bamboo. Cane is used primarily to make sugar and molasses, but can be eaten as a fruit.

West Indian browning sauce ▪ A molasses used to color and caramelize meat dishes.

Sweet potato ▪ Originally from Central and South America. Commonly used in Caribbean cooking. It can be boiled, baked, fried, or creamed.

Yam ▪ Similar in shape and size to a sweet potato, but with a nuttier flavor. Served boiled, mashed, or baked.

Caribbean Spices

Allspice ▪ A reddish-brown berry that is dried and used ground or whole in main dishes and desserts.

Bay rum tree ▪ The leaves of this tree are used to flavor soups, stews, and blaff (see Caribbean Foods, page 139).

Cinnamon ▪ Made from the bark of an evergreen tree. The best cinnamon is made by rolling the inner bark into quills or cylinders. It is used in many desserts and teas.

Cloves ▪ The dried buds of the clove tree. Used to add a spicy tang to fruit dishes and beverages.

Cumin ▪ One of the spices used in making curry powder. In the Caribbean, it is called jeera.

Curry ▪ A compound of different spices used principally by the Caribbean West Indians. It is made from ground cumin, chili powder, ginger, garam masala, coriander, turmeric, cardamom, and other spices.

Ginger ▪ The crushed root of the ginger plant, boiled with sugar to make a tea, soothes stomachaches.

Mace ▪ Grown mainly in Grenada, mace is the covering around the nutmeg (see below) and is dried and used as a flavoring.

Nutmeg ▪ A hard brown nut that is ground or grated for use in many dishes and desserts.

Scotch bonnet peppers ▪ A hot spicy pepper grown in the Caribbean.

Turmeric ▪ The dried, pulverized stem of a bright yellow plant that is a cousin of the ginger plant. Used as a powder and spice as well as a dye.

Caribbean Herbs
and Other Plants

Aloe ▪ Also known as *sinkle bible* in Jamaica. The bitter, viscous liquid that drips from its rubbery leaves is used to treat burns, sunburn, and warts; when diluted, it's used as an eyewash. Aloe originated in southern Africa; legend has it that Adam and Eve stole it from the Garden of Eden.

Arrowroot ▪ Starchy flour made from the root of the plant of the same name. Often used to make a special teething biscuit for babies and to thicken sauces and soups.

Breadfruit ▪ The leaves are used to treat headaches when applied directly to the forehead or taken as a tea.

Cerasee ▪ A wild vine that produces an orange fruit. Tea made from the leaves is used for colds and stomach pains.

Chainy root ▪ When boiled and mixed with other roots, it makes a bittersweet tonic that's rich in healthful minerals.

Fever grass ▪ Also known as lemon grass or lemon oil grass, it is used to flavor some curried foods and in perfume and as a medicinal tea for fevers and colds.

Khus khus ▪ A fragrant grass used to make perfume.

Pawpaw/papaya leaf ▪ Meat is wrapped in these leaves to make it tender.

Pepper elder ▪ Tea made from these leaves relieves gastric problems, indigestion, and flatulence.

Thyme ▪ Grows as a shrub; used in fish and meat dishes and in soups.

Caribbean Recipes

Curried Squash

Ingredients

1 tablespoon coriander seeds

1/4 cup (60 ml) cumin

1 medium dried pepper

1 cup (240 ml) chicken stock

1 1/2 pounds (675 g) winter squash or pumpkin, seeds removed

olive oil (for sautéing)

1 tablespoon (15 ml) minced onion

one clove garlic

1 tablespoon (15 ml) curry

cooked rice

1. In a dry, heavy skillet, toast coriander seeds with cumin.
2. Place coriander and cumin mixture in a blender with dried pepper and chicken stock. Blend.
3. Remove seeds from squash and cut squash into bite-size pieces.
4. Heat the oil and add the onion, garlic, and curry.
5. Cook, stirring constantly, for about 4 minutes.
6. Add the other ingredients and cook for about 25 minutes.
7. Serve over rice.

Caribbean Carrot Sticks

Ingredients

3 cups (720 ml) raw carrot sticks

2 tablespoons (30 ml) brown sugar

1/4 teaspoon (1.25 ml) ginger

1/8 cup (30 ml) orange juice mixed with 1/8 cup (30 ml) grapefruit juice

salt and pepper

1. Put all ingredients in a saucepan.
2. Cover and simmer until the carrots are tender.
3. Add salt and pepper to taste.

Coconut Rice

Ingredients

2 cups (480 ml) white rice

2 cups (480 ml) coconut water or milk

one cinnamon stick

two whole cloves

salt to taste

nutmeg (optional)

1. Rinse the rice twice. Drain.
2. Put the rice into a pan with coconut milk, spices, and salt. Bring to a boil.
3. Cook uncovered until the liquid evaporates.
4. Cover with a lid and simmer until tender.
5. Grate some nutmeg over the rice before serving.

© 1997 Fearon Teacher Aids

Soft Banana Pie

Ingredients

4 mashed ripe bananas

5 tablespoons (75 ml) brown sugar

juice of one lemon

1/2 teaspoon (2.5 ml) ground cinnamon

1 teaspoon (5 ml) powdered or fresh ground ginger

1/2 cup (120 ml) fine, dry wheat bread crumbs

3 eggs, beaten

2 cups (480 ml) hot milk

1. Mix the bananas, half the sugar, the juice, cinnamon, and ginger in an oven-proof pie pan; cover with bread crumbs.
2. Beat the eggs and the rest of the sugar; add the milk slowly.
3. Mix thoroughly and pour over the banana mixture.
4. Place the pie dish into a larger dish three-quarters filled with hot water and bake at 350°F (175°C) until set.

Channa Nibbles (an easy Jamaican snack)

Ingredients

1 cup (240 ml) vegetable oil

4 cups (960 ml) chickpeas, soaked overnight; or 2 cups (480 ml) canned chickpeas, drained and patted dry

1/2 teaspoon (2.5 ml) chili powder or red-pepper powder

salt to taste

1. Pour vegetable oil into skillet and set temperature at medium heat.
2. Add the chickpeas to the oil and brown the chickpeas.
3. Drain the chickpeas on paper towels. Sprinkle with chili powder and salt.
4. Eat the chickpeas while they are hot or place them in a tin can or other airtight container until it's time for the party.

Peas and Rice

Ingredients

1 or more tablespoons (15+ ml) margarine

4 cups (960 ml) cooked white rice

2 cups (480 ml) canned red kidney beans or green peas

1 medium onion

2 cloves garlic, crushed

1 cinnamon stick or 1 teaspoon (5 ml) ground cinnamon

1. Heat margarine in a heavy skillet.
2. Add rice, beans, and other ingredients and sauté until heated through.

Caribbean Orange Cups

Ingredients

1 Caribbean orange per child, available from specialty markets (the skin of these oranges is green or yellow when ripe)

1. Peel the orange by cutting off the skin, leaving the white pith.
2. Stand the orange on one end and slice one end almost off, leaving a little of the skin attached as a "hinge."
3. Place the orange in the refrigerator until chilled.
4. When you are ready to have a drink, soften the orange by rolling it back and forth between your hands.

Conkies

Ingredients

1 1/2 cups (360 ml) freshly chopped coconut or packaged coconut

2 cups (480 ml) fresh milk

2 cups (480 ml) finely ground cornmeal

1/2 cup (120 ml) raisins

green corn husks, banana leaves, or aluminum foil

1. Mix the coconut with the milk in a blender.

2. Mix the cornmeal with the raisins in a bowl.

3. Add the coconut-milk mixture to the cornmeal mixture. Combine thoroughly.

4. Use corn husks, banana leaves, or foil to make pockets for holding the mixture.

5. Spoon 2 tablespoons (30 ml) of batter into each pocket and wrap. Tuck in at edges and ends to make a partial seal.

6. Wrap string or thread around each package.

7. Place the packages in a pot of boiling water and simmer for about an hour.

8. Remove the packages from the pot, unwrap, and serve the cooked custard while it is hot.

Caribbean Gingerbread

Ingredients

1/2 cup (120 ml) molasses

1 cup (240 ml) sugar

1/2 cup (120 ml) butter

1/2 cup (120 ml) hot water

2 cups (480 ml) all-purpose flour, sifted

2 teaspoons (10 ml) baking powder

1/2 teaspoon (2.5 ml) salt

1 teaspoon (5 ml) nutmeg, freshly grated

2 teaspoons (10 ml) ginger root, freshly grated

1 egg, beaten

1. Preheat oven to 300°F (150°C) or use a slow-cooker crock pot with bread pan.
2. If using the oven, grease a 9-inch (22.5-cm) square pan and line with wax paper or lightly flour. For the slow cooker, grease the bread pan.
3. Gently heat the molasses, sugar, and butter in a medium pan over low heat. Stir in the hot water, then set aside.
4. Sift together the flour, baking powder, salt, and nutmeg in a medium bowl. Stir in the ginger root.
5. Add the egg.
6. Blend in the molasses mixture. Pour into prepared pan.
7. Bake in the oven for 1 hour or until cake tester comes out done; cool, then cut into nine squares. Set the slow cooker on High, place the bread pan in the slow cooker and cover the top of the can with eight paper towels. Bake for 3 to 4 hours. When done, let can cool for 5 minutes, then unmold gingerbread onto a cake rack.

Caribbean Fruit Delight

Mix together as many Caribbean fruits as possible, including bananas, peeled and sliced oranges, mangoes, pawpaws (papayas), pineapples, and guavas. Garnish with freshly grated coconut. Sprinkle with lemon juice to keep fruit from turning brown.

Roti

Ingredients

2 cups (480 ml) flour

1 teaspoon (5 ml) salt

1 teaspoon (5 ml) baking powder

2 tablespoons (30 ml) unsalted butter, softened

2/3 cup (158 ml) ice water

vegetable oil

1. Beat the first four ingredients together.
2. Add the ice water.
3. Form the mixture into a ball. Cover with a clean kitchen towel and set aside for 45 minutes.
4. Turn out the dough onto a floured surface and knead for 3 minutes.
5. Divide the dough into 12 equal portions. Roll each portion as thin as possible, oil each side, then cook in a heavy oiled skillet (about one minute per side).
6. Keep loaves warm in a towel.

Serve roti with meat, curry, creamed tuna, or sliced cooked potatoes with curry.

Pumpkin or Winter Squash Curry

Ingredients

3 tablespoons (45 ml) vegetable oil

1 medium onion

2 garlic cloves, chopped

2 tablespoons (30 ml) curry powder

1 1/2 pounds (675 g) winter squash or pumpkin, seeded and cut into bite-sized pieces

2 tomatoes or 1 can of tomatoes

1 sliced bell pepper

1 cup (240 ml) chicken stock

cooked rice

1. Heat the oil in a heavy skillet and add the onion, garlic, and curry.
2. Cook, stirring, for about 5 minutes.
3. Add the other ingredients and cook for about 25 minutes.
4. Serve over rice.

Pepper Pot

Cassava was once added to keep this soup from spoiling. Modern refrigeration now makes it unnecessary.

Ingredients

1 stewing chicken

4 pounds (1.8 kg) beef

4 pounds (1.8 kg) pork

1 oxtail

2 cloth bags, one with 3 tablespoons (45 ml) whole cloves, another with 6 whole chilies

cold water

4 teaspoons (20 ml) brown sugar

salt

cooked rice or sweet potatoes

1. Cut chicken into large pieces and place in a stainless steel or clay pot.
2. Cut beef, pork, and oxtail into 2 inch (5 cm) pieces; add to pot.
3. Tie the clove and chili bags to the pot handles so that the bags hang inside the pot. Cover the meats and spice bags with cold water.
4. Add salt and brown sugar, and simmer until the meat falls off the bones.
5. Serve over rice or boiled and sliced sweet potatoes.

Fried Plantain

Ingredients

4 ripe plantains (or bananas, if you can't get plantains)

4 tablespoons (60 ml) vegetable oil

salt

1. Peel the plantains and cut them once lengthwise and once crosswise (into four pieces).
2. Heat the oil in a large heavy skillet over medium heat.
3. Fry the plantain pieces on each side until golden brown.

© 1997 Fearon Teacher Aids

Soursop Punch

Ingredients

2 soursops (see Caribbean Foods, page 140), peeled and seeded

1 cup (240 ml) milk

2 tablespoons (30 ml) sugar

ice cubes

1. Put the peeled and seeded soursops in a blender with the milk, sugar, and ice.
2. Pulse the blender on "liquefy" setting for two minutes.
3. Serve in tall glasses.

Barbecue Marinade

The hot dogs in this recipe are a close approximation to the heavily smoked and dehydrated beef jerky that pirates once cooked over open fires.

Ingredients

1 Scotch bonnet or chili pepper, seeded and cored

1 onion, sliced

2 celery stalks, chopped

2 cloves garlic, mashed

1 teaspoon (5 ml) salt

1 teaspoon (5 ml) brown sugar

1 teaspoon (5 ml) ground allspice

1 teaspoon (5 ml) ground nutmeg

1 teaspoon (5 ml) ground cinnamon

1 teaspoon (5 ml) fresh-ground pepper

2 teaspoons (10 ml) cider vinegar

hot dogs

1. Mix the first eleven ingredients together in a bowl.
2. Add the hot dogs and let them soak in the marinade at room temperature overnight.
3. Grill the hot dogs, brushing them frequently with the marinade as they cook.

Cornmeal Cou Cou

Ingredients

1 1/3 cups (320 ml) cornmeal

1 cup (240 ml) cold water

7 medium-sized okras, sliced thin

2 cups (480 ml) boiling water

3/4 teaspoon (3.75 ml) salt

butter to taste

1. Mix the cornmeal with the cold water until smooth.
2. Cook the okra in boiling water for about five minutes.
3. Reduce heat and add the salt and cornmeal batter, stirring constantly.
4. When the mixture is stiff, place it in a buttered dish. Make a little hole, or "nest," on top for the butter.

Ensalada de Atun desde Puerto Rico
(Puerto Rican Tuna Salad)

Ingredients

2 heads lettuce, washed and dried

2 6- or 7-ounce cans (168 or 196 g) tuna fish, flaked

2 sliced or sectioned oranges

2 cups (480 ml) fresh or canned pineapple, cut into cubes

1 lime, quartered

2 tablespoons (30 ml) chopped coriander

1/4 cup (60 ml) olive oil

salt and pepper

1. On a plate, arrange lettuce leaves to form four "lettuce cups." Place tuna, oranges, and pineapple inside each cup.
2. Sprinkle the salad cups with lime juice, coriander, oil, salt, and pepper.
3. Serve immediately.

Stamp and Go, or Accras—
Jamaica, Martinique

Ingredients

1/2 cup (120 ml) dried salt cod

cold water

1/2 cup (120 ml) flour

1/2 teaspoon (2.5 ml) baking powder

1 lightly beaten egg

2 tablespoons (30 ml) ice water

1 chopped onion

1 clove garlic

1 small hot pepper, seeded and cored

vegetable oil

1. Soak the fish in the cold water for 24 hours.
2. Mix all the other ingredients (except the oil) together and pour over the fish.
3. Heat the oil in a heavy pan to 375°F (190°C).
4. Fry one tablespoon of the fish mixture at a time, on both sides.
5. Remove from oil with a slotted spoon and drain on paper towels. Serve hot.

(Note: Accras is also made with other seafood or vegetables.)

Fufu—Jamaica

Ingredients

4 green bananas or plantains

boiling water

3 tablespoons (45 ml) soft butter

salt and pepper to taste

1. Boil bananas in their skins for 30 minutes to tenderize.
2. Peel bananas and mash with a mortar, or mix in a blender or food processor until smooth.
3. Blend in butter, salt, and pepper.
4. Form batter into little cakes and place on a cookie sheet.
5. Bake three to five minutes in 375°F (190°C) oven.

Fluff Dumplings—Jamaica

Ingredients

3/4 cup (180 ml) flour

1/5 teaspoon (1 ml) salt

1/4 cup (60 ml) soda water (club soda)

1 cup (240 ml) crushed peanuts

boiling water

1. Sift the flour and salt into a bowl.
2. Slowly add the soda.
3. Mix to form a stiff dough.
4. Shape the dough into six small balls. Pressing firmly, roll the dough balls in the crushed peanuts.
5. Place the dumplings into the boiling water for 12 to 15 minutes until cooked.

Bajan Cakes—Barbados

Ingredients

3/4 cup (75 g) flour

1 teaspoon (5 ml) baking powder

1 teaspoon (5 ml) sugar

2 tablespoons (30 ml) margarine

1/3 cup (79 ml) ice water

green sugar for decoration (see recipe, below)

1. Sift the dry ingredients into a bowl; cut in the margarine with a fork.
2. Slowly add the ice water.
3. Stir until the batter forms a sticky dough.
4. Knead lightly on a floured board.
5. Let the dough rest for up to half an hour.
6. Form the dough into the shape of a stalk of sugar cane.
7. Sprinkle with green sugar.
8. Place the cane stalk on a greased cookie sheet and bake at 375°F (190°C) for about 20 minutes.

To Make Green Sugar

Add a few drops of food coloring to refined white sugar and stir. Store sugar in airtight container for at least 24 hours before using.

Language Glossaries
French

Alfabet
Pronunciation

A	B	C	D	E	F	G	H	I
(ah)	(bay)	(say)	(day)	(ay)	(ehf)	(zhay)	(ahsh)	(ee)

J	K	L	M	N	O	P	Q	R
(zhee)	(kah)	(ehll)	(ehm)	(ehn)	(oh)	(pay)	(koo)	(ehrr)

S	T	U	V	W	X	Y	Z
(ehs)	(tay)	(oo)	(vay)	(DOO bluh vay)	(eeks)	(ee grehk)	(zehd)

Nasal Vowels

un	(uh<u>n</u>)
bon	(oh<u>n</u>)
vin	(a<u>n</u>)
blanc	(ah<u>n</u>)

Un bon vin blanc (a good white wine) is pronounced like this:
(uh<u>n</u> boh<u>n</u> va<u>n</u> blah<u>n</u>k).

Important Words and Questions

French	English	Pronunciation
Quoi?	What?	(kwah)
Pourquoi?	Why?	(poor KWAH)
Qui?	Who?	(kee)
Combien?	How much?	(koh<u>n</u> bee AN)
Quel(le)?	Which?	(kehl)
Où	Where?	(oo)
Comment?	How?	(KOH mah<u>n</u>)
Quand?	When?	(kah<u>n</u>)
Comment allez-vous?	How are you?	(KOH mah<u>n</u>t AH lay voo)
Quel est votre nom?	What is your name?	(kehl eh VOH truh noh<u>n</u>)
Où est . . .	Where is . . .	(oo eh)
. . . un hôtel?	. . . a hotel?	(uh<u>n</u> oh TEHL)
. . . un restaurant?	. . . a restaurant?	(uh<u>n</u> rehs toh RAH<u>N</u>)
. . . la poste de police?	. . . the police station?	(la pohst de poh LEES)

Oui	Yes	(wee)
Non	No	(no<u>h</u>n)
A bientôt	See you later.	(ah bee A<u>N</u> toh)
Au revoir	Goodbye	(oh ruh VWAHR)
Bonjour	Good day, hello	(bo<u>h</u>n ZHOOR)
Merci	Thank you.	(mehr SEE)
Je ne parle pas français.	I don't speak French.	(zhuh nuh pahrl pah frah<u>n</u> SAY)

Désolé.	I'm sorry.	(DAY zoh lay)
S'il vous plaît	Please	(see voo play)
Bienvenu!	Welcome!	(bee A<u>N</u> veh noo)
Je m'appelle . . .	My name is . . .	(zhuh mah PEHL)

Les aliments • Food

le sel ▪ salt
le poivre ▪ pepper
le beurre ▪ butter
le fromage ▪ cheese
le lait ▪ milk
la crème ▪ cream
le café ▪ coffee
le thé ▪ tea
le pain ▪ bread
le poulet ▪ chicken
le poisson ▪ fish
le jambon ▪ ham
le porc ▪ pork
le boeuf ▪ beef
la pomme de terre ▪ potato
la laitue ▪ lettuce
le dessert ▪ dessert
la boisson ▪ beverage
le petit déjeuner ▪ breakfast
le déjeuner ▪ lunch
le dîner ▪ dinner

La bijouterie • Jewelry

la bague ▪ ring
les boucles d'oreille ▪ earrings
la chaînette ▪ chain
le collier ▪ necklace
le bracelet ▪ bracelet
la montre ▪ watch
l'épingle ▪ pin

Les vêtements • Clothes

le chemisier ▪ blouse
les bottes ▪ boots
la chemise ▪ shirt
le sac à main ▪ purse
le veston ▪ jacket
la ceinture ▪ belt
la jupe ▪ skirt
le chapeau ▪ hat
la robe ▪ dress
les chaussures ▪ shoes
les chaussettes ▪ socks
le pantalon ▪ pants

Spanish

Alfabeto
Pronounciation

A (ah)	B (bay)	C (say)	CH (say AH chay)	D (day)	E (eh)
F (EF eh)	G (heh)	H (AH chay)	I (ee)	J (HOH tah)	K (kah)
L (EHL eh)	LL (EH yeh)	M (EHM eh)	N (EHN eh)	Ñ (EHN ee eh)	O (oh)
P (peh)	Q (koo)	R (EHR reh)	RR (DOB ler EHR reh)	S (EHS eh)	T (tay)
U (oo)	V (bay)	X (DOB leh bay)	Y (EHK ees)	W (ee GREE eh ga)	Z (ZAY tah)

Important Words and Questions

Spanish	English	Pronunciation
¿Qué?	What?	(kay)
¿Por qué?	Why?	(pohr kay)
(porque = "because")		
¿Quién?	Who?	(kee EHN)
¿Cuántos?	How much? or How many?	(KWAHN tohs)
¿Cuál?	Which?	(kwahl)
¿Dónde?	Where?	(DAWN day)
¿De dónde?	From where?	(day DAWN day)
¿Adónde?	To where?	(ah DAWN day)
¿Cómo?	How?	(KOH moh)
¿Cuándo?	When?	(KWAHN doh)
¿Cómo está?	How are you?	(KOH moh ehs TAH)
¿Cómo se llama?	What is your name?	(KOH moh say YAH mah)
¿Dónde está . . .	Where is . . .	(DOHN day ehs TAH)
. . . un hotel?	. . . a hotel?	(oon oh TEHL)
. . . un restaurante?	. . . a restaurant?	(oon rehs tow RAHN teh)

© 1997 Fearon Teacher Aids

Spanish	English	Pronunciation
. . . la comisaría?	. . . the police station?	(lah koh mee sah REE ah)
Sí	Yes	(see)
No	No	(noh)
Hasta la vista.	See you later.	(AH stah lah VEES tah)
Adiós	Goodbye	(ah dee OHS)
Buenos días	Good day	(BWAY nohs DEE ahs)
Hola	Hello	(OH lah)
Gracias	Thank you	(GRAH see ahs)
No hablo español.	I don't speak Spanish.	(noh AH bloh ehs pah NYOHL)
Lo siento.	I'm sorry.	(loh see EHN toh)
Por favor	Please	(pohr fah VOHR)
¡Bien venidos!	Welcome!	(bee EHN veh NEE dohs)
Me llamo . . .	My name is . . .	(may YAH moh)

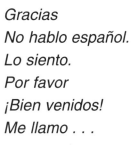

La comida • Food

- la sal • salt
- la pimienta • pepper
- la mantequilla • butter
- el queso • cheese
- la leche • milk
- la crema • cream
- el café • coffee
- el té • tea
- el pan • bread
- el pollo • chicken
- el pescado • fish
- el jamón • ham
- la carne de puerco • pork
- la carne de res • beef
- la papa • potato
- la lechuga • lettuce
- el postre • dessert
- las bebidas • beverages
- el desayuno • breakfast
- la comida • lunch
- la cena • dinner

Las joyas • Jewelry

- el anillo • ring
- los aretes • earrings
- la cadena • chain
- el collar • necklace
- el dije • charm
- la pulsera • bracelet
- el reloj • watch

La ropa • Clothes

- la blusa • blouse
- las botas • boots
- la bufanda • scarf
- el calcetín • sock
- la camisa • shirt
- la cartera • purse
- la chaqueta • jacket
- el cinturón • belt
- la falda • skirt
- el sombrero • hat
- el vestido • dress
- los zapatos • shoes

Creole
Jamaican Creole or patois (patwa)

arm-strick ▪ crutch

backra, buckra ▪ white person; whites; in slave days, term used to address white master

bankra ▪ basket

banggarang ▪ great noise or disturbance

batty ▪ backside

bex ▪ vex or vexed

blind oat(h) ▪ a lie

bra ▪ brother

bredda ▪ brother

bride ▪ woman about to be married or who is newly married, but can also refer to bridegroom

bring come ▪ bring it here

bulla ▪ small sugar cake

cranky ▪ sickly, in poor health

cris ▪ "crisp," top-notch, superlative

dege-dege ▪ small, skimpy, as in portions

downpressor ▪ oppressor

dutchie ▪ heavy cooking pot

foot ▪ can refer to any part of the leg from the foot to the thigh

galliwasp ▪ lizard that was often the subject of folk tales, incorrectly assumed to be poisonous

good-belly ▪ good natured, kindly

hackle ▪ hassle, worry

hard ▪ old; also skilled

I and I, I 'n' I ▪ we

in (one's) ackee ▪ feeling fit, energetic

irie ▪ state of goodness, something good; now commonly used throughout the country to mean "fine"

I-tal ▪ natural foods and method of preparing food; natural life

langa ▪ shrimp or crayfish

Kiss me neck! ▪ exclamation of surprise

labrish ▪ gossip

maga ▪ thin

make ▪ allow, permit, as in "make a see," or "let me see"

mash ▪ smash, crush, destroy

nyam ▪ eat

ongle ▪ only

pear ▪ avocado pear

pickney ▪ child, derived from *pickaninny*, a denigrating word used for black children in slavery days

quashie ▪ foolish, stupid person

ratchet ▪ knife

roots ▪ natural, approved African ways and values

site up ▪ to see

Trinidadian Creole

It make hot ▪ I'm hot

It have ▪ There is, there are

doo doo ▪ honey, sweetheart

parang ▪ Christmas music

© 1997 Fearon Teacher Aids

Capsule Rasta Talk

Armageddon ▪ the final battle between good and evil as predicted in the Bible

aks ▪ ask

bakra ▪ white slavemaster, or member of the ruling class in colonial days ("back raw")

bammy ▪ pancake made of cassava (after cassava has been grated and the bitter juice removed by squeezing)

callalou ▪ spinach stew

deddes ▪ meat

dreadnut ▪ coconut

dunza, dunzai ▪ money

fire, fiyah ▪ Rasta greeting

first light ▪ tomorrow

first night ▪ last night

fullness ▪ state of being full, absolute, complete

gates ▪ Rasta home or yard

groundation ▪ large Rasta gathering

hail ▪ a greeting

I 'n' I ▪ I, we

i-tal ▪ natural foods, wholesome cooking, purity, natural style of life

ingman ▪ husband

irate ▪ create

isire, izire ▪ desire

itches ▪ matches

ites ▪ Rasta greeting meaning "may the receiver attain spiritual heights"

iwer ▪ power

Jah-Mak-Ya, Jamdung, Ja, Jamdown ▪ Jamaica

Kiss me neck! ▪ ordinary exclamation of surprise

little more, more time ▪ see you later

no true? ▪ isn't it so?

one love ▪ parting expression meaning unity

paki ▪ calabash

pollution ▪ the masses of humanity living in spiritual darkness

rat-bat ▪ bat (flying rodent)

roots ▪ Rasta greeting; native, natural, derived from communal experience

sidung ▪ sit down

smadi ▪ somebody

upfull ▪ upright

vex ▪ to get angry

wh'appen ▪ what's happening?

yood ▪ food

Zion ▪ mythical Africa; Ethiopia

Caribbean Indian Languages

Listed below are what are thought to be Caribbean Indian words that have been incorporated into the English language, having come down to us through the early Spanish-speaking explorers and settlers.

Arawakan

caniba or *carib* ▪ cannibal

guana or *guano* ▪ iguana

guayaba or *guayabo* ▪ guava

Taino

barbacoa ▪ barbecue

batata ▪ sweet potato

batata or *patata* ▪ potato

caçábi ▪ cassava

guiro ▪ percussion instrument

hamaca ▪ hammock

huracan, hurakán, furacane, or *hurricano* ▪ hurricane

maize ▪ corn

mangrove ▪ mangrove

sabana, savanna, savannah ▪ savanna

tobaco ▪ tobacco

yuca or *juca* ▪ cassava or yucca

Cariban

annatto ▪ red dyestuff

caiman or *cayman* ▪ reptile

canoa or *canaua* ▪ canoe

cassiri ▪ fermented drink

curare, oorali, or *urali* ▪ curare (a poison)

manatee ▪ manatee

pecari or *peccary* ▪ wild pig

tamarin ▪ marmoset (a small monkey)

Literal Translations of Caribbean Indian Terms

"heavenly plume of feathers" ▪ rainbow

"my heart" ▪ wife

"makes little children for me" ▪ son-in-law

"boiling pot" ▪ earthquake

"daddy of the fingers" ▪ thumb

"funny-shaped enemy" ▪ European

Sailing Terms

aft ▪ at or near the stern, or the back, of the boat

aloft ▪ high up on the mast or rigging

anchor ▪ a strong, heavy device, frequently made of iron, that grips the sea bottom to restrict a boat's motion. It is fastened to the boat with a chain.

"Anchor's aweigh!" ▪ an exclamation meaning the "anchor has been raised and the ship is ready to sail away."

ashore ▪ at port, in the harbor, or on the shore

bail ▪ to scoop water from the bottom of the boat with a bucket

barnacle ▪ small hard-shelled marine animals that attach to ship bottoms, piers, rocks, and so on

batten ▪ to secure firmly, as in "batten down the hatches"

beach ▪ the shore

beam ▪ the width of the ship at its widest point

below ▪ under the deck or decks of a ship

berth ▪ a bunk or bed on a ship

bow ▪ the forward part of a vessel

bridge ▪ the navigation deck

cabin ▪ living quarters

capsize ▪ to turn over

compass ▪ device used to determine direction. It has a magnetized needle that points north.

deck ▪ a floor of a ship

ebb ▪ the falling tide

flood ▪ a great overflow of water; the rising tide

galley ▪ a ship's kitchen

guardrail ▪ a framework of metal bars around the outside of the deck, forming a support or barrier to prevent a person from falling over the ship's side

gunwales ▪ the topmost part of a boat's sides

hatch ▪ an opening in a ship's deck or the cover over such an opening

head ▪ the ship's toilet

heave-to ▪ to slow or stop a boat using its sails and rudder

hull ▪ the lowermost part of a ship; its frame or main body

jack ▪ a small national flag flown on a ship's bow

jetty ▪ a wall that restrains water currents to protect a harbor; also a pier or wharf

jib ▪ a triangular sail in front of the mast

keel ▪ main fore-to-aft timber in the bottom of a ship's hull

knot ▪ the unit of speed used by ships and boats; 1 knot equals 1 nautical mile per hour

ladder ▪ a stairway aboard ship

leeward ▪ the direction that the wind is blowing toward; going with the wind

log ▪ the written record of a ship's voyage or trip

mast ▪ a tall, stout pole that rises above the deck of a ship to hold the sails, spars, and rigging

pennant ▪ a narrow, triangular flag, sometimes used to signal other ships

port ▪ the left side of a boat

rigging ▪ the ropes, chains, and tackle used to make a ship's sails and masts work

slip ▪ a parking place for a boat

spar ▪ a stout pole that is used as a vertical mast or horizontally to hold a ship's sails

starboard ▪ the right side of a boat

stern ▪ the back of the boat

tack ▪ a sailing ship's direction that is determined by the wind direction; one part of a ship's zigzag movement as it proceeds to windward

tacking ▪ turning a boat's bow into and across the wind

tackle ▪ equipment on a ship that uses pulleys to lift, lower, or shift the position of sails, spars, and so on

toe rail ▪ the part of a boat on the main deck that stops a person's feet from sliding over the side of the boat

windward ▪ the direction from which the wind blows; going toward the wind

Music and Musical Instruments

Anancy and Cow

African folk song transported to Jamaica
Arranged by Richard Judd

"Anancy" refers to an African character that is prominent in Jamaican folklore. Anancy was half spider and half human. The name comes from the Ashanti word meaning "spider." This fellow is usually portrayed as a lazy, selfish, and greedy person who, in this song, shows how he traps his victims by tying them up with his web. The words *me no min know de bad me do* means "I didn't know the bad thing I did."

Firmly

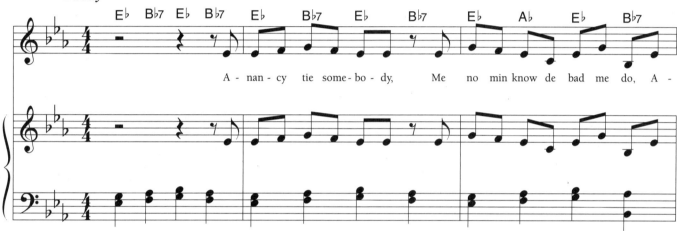

Add a steady-beat rhythm accompaniment to the song, using claps or other body percussion. See rhythm pattern below.

Hand claps

Boston Come All Ye

Sea Chantey
Arranged by Richard Judd

1. Come all ye young sailors and listen to me, __ I'll sing you a song of the fish in the sea.
2. Oh, first came the shale, __ the biggest of all, __ He climbed up a loft and let fish ev'ry sail fall.
3. And next came the mackerel with his striped back, __ He hauled aft the sheets __ and boarded each tack.
4. And then came the smelt, __ the smallest of all: __ He jumped to the poop and sang out, "Top-sail haul!"
5. Oh, last came the flounder as flat as the ground. __ Says, "Blast your eyes chuckle-head, mind how you sound!"

REFRAIN

Then blow ye winds west-er-ly, west-er-ly blow. __ We're bound to the South-'ard, so stead-y she goes.

Chantey melody from EXPLORING MUSIC, Grade 5, Pupil's Edition. Published by Holt, Rinehart and Winston, Inc.

Hosanna

Calypso from Jamaica
Arranged by Richard Judd

Building a house in Jamaica is a ceremonious, almost religious occasion. This song is a
house builder's song that is based on the parable of the wise man and the foolish man.
Only the wise man's house remains standing despite rain, sunshine, breezes, and storms.
Jamaican house builders often sing this song repeating the first phrase (*Hosanna! Me
build a house!*) until they finish a specific task.

1. Ho - san-na, me build a house, oh___ Ho - san-na, me build a house, oh___ Ho - san-na, me build a house, oh,___ I built it on the sand-y ground. Me house built on a sand-y ground. It will fall you
2. Ho - san-na, me build a house, oh___ Ho - san-na, me build a house, oh___ Ho - san-na, me build a house, oh,___ I built it on the sol - id ground. Me house built on a sol - id ground. It will stand you

house can nev-er___ be, No! No! Me house too weak you___ see, No! No! Me
house will ev-er___ be, Yes! Yes! Me house too strong you___ see, Yes! Yes! Me

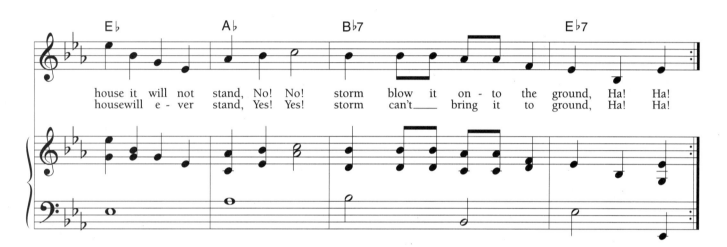

house it will not stand, No! No! storm blow it on-to the ground, Ha! Ha!
house will e-ver stand, Yes! Yes! storm can't___ bring it to ground, Ha! Ha!

Here are several calypso rhythm patterns to try. Use a few of them to create a rhythmic ostinato (a repeating pattern) for the song. This will add an authenic touch to the song's accompaniment. The percussion instruments indicated (made in class or purchased) or body percussion (hand clapping, finger snapping, finger tapping, thigh tapping, toe tapping, and so on) may be used.

Calypso rhythm patterns

The *John B.* Sails

Folk Song from the Bahamas
Arranged by Richard Judd

This Bahamian folk song might be fun to sing during Regatta while pretending to be sailors on a sloop (a sailboat with a single mast).

night
lone
home,

Just see - in' the sights,
And let___ me go home,
I want___ to go home,

Well, I feel so break___ up,___   I want___ to go
Well, I feel so break___ up,___   I want___ to go
Well, this is the worst___ trip___ Since I___ was

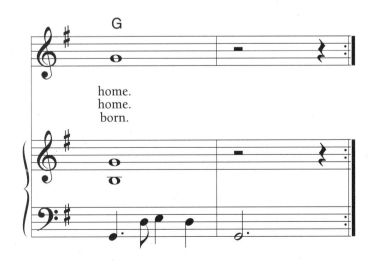

home.
home.
born.

Musical Instruments

See also Calabash Maracas (p. 103) and Bamboo Chimes (p. 90).

Maracas

The most natural maraca is the gourd. When completely dry (which can take several months), the outside of the gourd will be very hard, and the seeds inside will make a rattling sound when shaken. If it is not possible to find gourds, use balloons covered with papier-mâché strips to make maracas.

Materials

- inflated balloon
- papier-mâché paste and strips
- paper towels or tissues
- scissors
- pebbles, beans, or seeds

- wooden dowel, 1/2 inch (1.25 cm) thick and 6 inches (15.25 cm) in length
- glue
- paint and paintbrushes
- spray shellac

1. Cover the balloon with papier-mâché and let it dry several days (last layer should be plain paper towels or tissues).

2. After it is completely dry, cut a small hole in the sphere and carefully pop and remove the balloon.

3. Drop pebbles, beans, or seeds into the dried sphere.

4. Test the fit of the dowel by placing it through the hole. Remove dowel, place glue on the insertion end and replace it in the hole. Add glue around the edges of the dowel where it enters the hole to secure it. Allow the glue to dry.

5. Decorate the maraca with paint, then let it dry.

6. Apply one or two coats of shellac to make the maraca shiny. Allow drying time between coats.

Sand Blocks

Rubbing one sandpaper surface against another sandpaper surface makes a sound that resembles the sound a soft-shoe dancer makes.

Materials

- 2 blocks of wood, 3 inches by 4 inches by 1 inch (8 cm x 10 cm x 2.5 cm)
- coarse sandpaper
- scissors
- tacks and hammer, or glue

1. Cut two pieces of sandpaper to a size that will fit around the wooden blocks.

2. Wrap one piece of sandpaper around each block and glue or tack it onto the underside of the block.

3. Rub the sandpaper blocks gently together to create a pleasant sound.

Stringed Box Guitar

Stretching rubber bands across a box is easy, and the resulting instrument makes a very soft sound that can add to some kinds of music. Note: It is not possible to tune the "strings" to any definite pitches. If you wish, try amplifying the sound if you have a karaoke or microphone and sound system in your classroom.

Materials

- tissue box or cigar box
- scissors
- masking tape
- white glue
- rubber bands of several weights
- 2 sticks, 1/2 inch by 1/2 inch by 3 inch (1.25 cm x 1.25 cm x 8 cm)

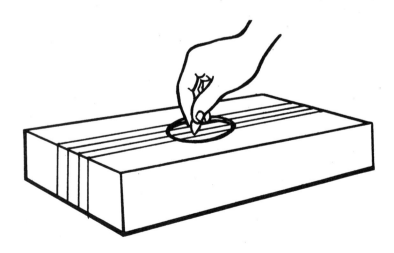

1. If using a cigar box, cut a hole in the top of the box to let the sound out. This side becomes the top of the guitar. Tape or glue the box lid securely to the sides.

2. If using a tissue box, the top of the box (where the tissue hole opening is) becomes the top of the guitar.

3. Stretch different-weight rubber bands across the hole and experiment as to what sounds can be made.

4. To allow rubber bands to resonate, raise the bands away from the surface of the box by inserting the two small sticks near the ends of the box and gluing them in place.

Claves

Find two hardwood sticks about 7 inches (18 cm) long. Smooth well with sandpaper. When the sticks are struck together, they will make a sharp sound.

Ankle Rattles

Materials

- bottle caps
- wooden block
- hammer
- nail
- strong twine
- jingle bells (optional)

1. Place the bottle caps on the block of wood and punch holes in them, using a hammer and nail.

2. String the punched caps on twine.

3. Small jingle bells may also be added to the bottle caps.

4. Tie around ankles to rattle when feet are stomped during dancing.

Hum Drums—Haiti

A hum drum is any kind of drum that is tapped while the drummer hums. One such drum could be large empty glass water bottles turned upside down. Even the Haitian dogs seem to like the drums, as they will wail and hum along with the hum drummers.

Bamba Drum

Almost anything can become a drum. By stretching a membrane across a can, which acts as a resonator, a drum is born. The best thing to use is thin leather; however, this may not be easy to find, so strong rubber sheeting will work as a substitute.

Materials

- gallon-size can (empty and clean)
- thin leather, chamois, or rubber sheeting
- scissors
- lengths of string

1. Remove at least one end of the can.

2. Cut a round piece of leather or rubber sheeting that will extend over the edge of the can by 2 inches (5 cm).

3. With the scissors, make eight or ten evenly spaced holes around the edge of the circle of leather or rubber.

4. Tie strings to four or five consecutive holes on one side of the circle.

5. Stretch the circle over the open end of the can.

6. Pull the strings down under the can one at a time and attach them to their opposite holes on the other side of the circle.

7. Extra strings can be used to make the skin taut.

An alternative: Stretch a membrane over a wooden nail keg and firmly tack in place around the edges.

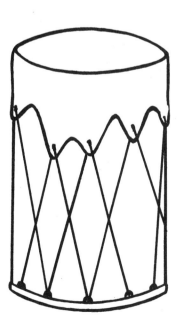

Tassa Drum—Trinidad

This kind of drum is used for the Hosay festival. It has a goatskin or membrane stretched across a clay coil pot and fastened around the pot with string, rubber bands, or strong twine. When the membrane is heated, it fits tighter, causing the pitch of the drum to rise. For the skin, light leather, a sheet of rubber, tough butcher paper, or a wet brown paper bag will work. The paper skins won't be as sturdy as leather or rubber, but if sprayed with several coats of shellac, they will firm up enough for gentle use.

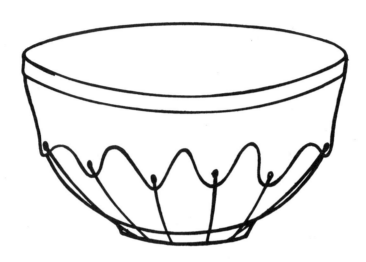

Flags

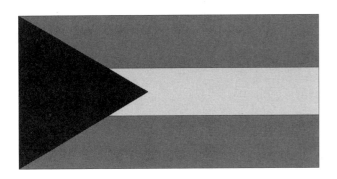

Bahamas

Barbados

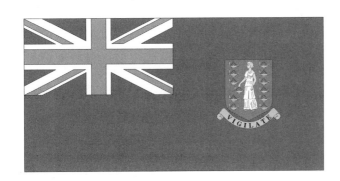

British Virgin Islands

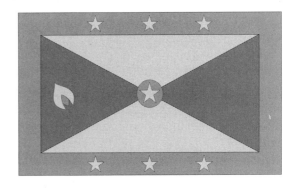

Grenada

Guadeloupe and Martinique

Flags

Haiti

Jamaica

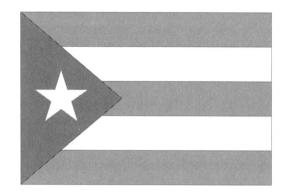

Puerto Rico

St. Vincent & the Grenadines

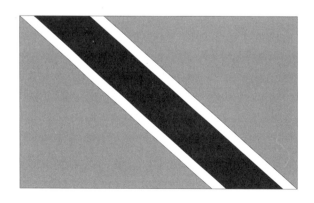

Trinidad and Tobago

Bibliography of Resources for Kids

The Amazing Potato: A Story in Which the Incas, Conquistadores, Marie Antoinette, Thomas Jefferson, Wars, Famines, Immigrants, and French Fries All Play a Part by Milton Meltzer. HarperCollins, 1992. (Grade 4 and up)

America the Beautiful: Puerto Rico by Deborah Kent. Children's, 1992. (Grade 4 and up)

Anansi the Spider retold by Gerald McDermott. Holt, 1986. Traditional African trickster in oral tradition of the Ashanti people of Ghana. (Grades 4–6)

Anansi, the Spider Man: Jamaican Folk Tales retold by Sir Philip Sherlock. Crowell, 1948. Ties in with the African folklore character and is part of the West Indian storytelling tradition. (Grades 4–6)

Animals of the Sea and Shore by Illa Podendorf. New True Book Series. Children's, 1982. (Grades 1–4)

The Audubon Society Field Guide to North American Fishes, Whales and Dolphins by Audubon Society Staff, et al. Knopf, 1983. (Grades K–8)

The Audubon Society Field Guide to North American Seashells by Audubon Society Staff and Harold A. Rehder. Knopf, 1981. (Grades K–8)

The Audubon Society Field Guide to North American Seashore Creatures by Audubon Society Staff and Norman A. Meinkoth. Knopf, 1981. (Grades K–8)

The Banza: A Haitian Story retold by Diana Wolkstein. Dial, 1981. A banza is an old African instrument like a banjo. (Grades K–3)

Beat the Story Drum, Pum-Pum by Ashley Bryan. Atheneum, 1980. Five African folk tales with the rhythm and idiom of the African oral tradition. (Grades 1–4)

Boat by Eric Kently. Knopf, 1992. Traces the historic development and uses of boats from rafts to luxury liners. (Grade 4 and up)

The Boy Who Sailed with Columbus by Michael Forman. Arcade, 1992. Fictional account of a boy left behind, with a skeleton crew, on one of the newly discovered islands to start a colony and to await Columbus's return. (Grades 3–5)

The Calypso Alphabet by John Agard. Holt, 1989. Illustrates Caribbean life and customs around alphabetically arranged words indigenous to the islands. (Grades K–2)

Caribbean by John Griffith. Countries of the World Series. Watts, 1989. (Grades 4–6)

Caribbean by Anthony Mason. People and Places Series. Silver Burdett Ginn, 1989. (Grade 4 and up)

Caribbean ABC by Marion Rogers. CRIC, 1992. (preschool–Grade 1)

Caribbean Alphabet by Frane Lessac. Tambourine, 1994. Images such as *h* for *hibiscus, m* for *mangoes, r* for *reggae.* (Grades K–4)

Caribbean Canvas by Frane Lessac. Wordsong, 1994 (reissue of 1987 title). Uses art and poetry to show island life and values. (All ages)

Caribbean Crosswords by A. Anduze. Eastern Caribbean Institute, 1994. (Grade 5 and up)

A Caribbean Dozen: Poems from Caribbean Poets edited by John Agard and Grace Nichols. Candlestick, 1994. Appreciation of nature and appreciation of life are emphasized. (Grades 4–6)

Caribbean Folk Legends by Theresa Lewis. Young Reader's Service. African World, 1990. (Grade 5 and up)

Caribbean Stories by Robert Hull. Tales from Around the World Series. Thomson Learning, 1994. (Grade 5 and up)

The Cat's Purr by Ashley Bryan. Atheneum, 1985. A West Indian folk tale. (Grades K–2)

The Cay by Theodore Taylor. Doubleday, 1987. A World War II freighter traveling from the United States to Curaçao is torpedoed and sunk. A racially prejudiced young white boy is marooned on a small coral island, or cay, with an old black man. A fierce tropical storm adds to the conflict. (Grades 4–6)

The Chalk Doll by Charlotte Pomerantz. Harper, 1993. (Grades K–3)

Christopher Columbus—A Great Explorer by Carol Greene. A Rookie Biography. Children's, 1989. (Grades K–3)

Christopher Columbus and the Great Voyage of Discovery by Jo Anne Weisman and Kenneth Deitch. Picture Book Biography Series, V. 1. Discovery Enterprises, 1990. (Grades 2–5)

Christopher Columbus: How He Did It by Charlotte Yue. Houghton, 1992. Answers many questions that students often ask. Meticulous drawings. (Grade 5 and up)

Coconut Kind of Day: Island Poems by Lynn Joseph. Puffin, 1992. (Grade 4 and up)

The Conch Book by Dee Carstarphen. Banyan, 1981. The queen conch, from gestation to gastronomy. (Grades K–6)

Coral Reef by Jane Burton. Dorling Kindersley, 1992. Seahorse, hermit crab, and sea slug are represented in this photographic examination of the variety of life found on coral reefs. (Grades 3–6)

Coral Reefs in Danger by Christopher Lampton. Millbrook, 1992. How a reef is formed, its ecosystem, and problems possibly caused by global warming. (Grade 4 and up)

Corals: The Sea's Great Builders by the Cousteau Society Staff. Cousteau Nature Adventure Books. Simon & Schuster, 1992. (Grades 1–5)

Crafts for Kwanzaa by Kathy Ross. Millbrook, 1994. Explains history of this holiday; includes ideas for gifts and decorations. (Grades 1–3)

Cuba by Anamaria Vazquez and Rosa Cases. Enchantment of America Series. Children's, 1987. (Grade 5 and up)

The Dancing Granny by Ashley Bryan. Aladdin, 1987. Indian folk tale in which traditional folk character, Spider Ananse, tries to trick Granny. (Grades 1–4)

Discovering Marine Mammals by Nancy Field and Sally Machlis. A Learning Activity Book. Dog-eared, 1987. (Grades 1–6)

Dolphins by Cousteau Society Staff. Little Simon Series. Simon & Schuster, 1992. (preschool–Grade 1)

Far-Flung America by Allen Carpenter. The New Enchantment of America Series. Children's, 1984. (Grade 4 and up)

Feliz Nochebuena, Feliz Navidad: Christmas Feasts of the Hispanic Caribbean by Presilla Maricel. Holt, 1994. (Grades 3–7)

Field Guide to the Birds of North America edited by Shirley Scott. National Geographic, 1987. (Grades K–8)

The Fire Children by Eric Maddern. Dial, 1993. West African creation tale about why skin colors vary. (Grades K–4)

Fish Facts and Fancies by Henry Berkowitz. Banyan. An educational coloring book. (Grades 1–6)

1492: The Year of the New World by Piero Ventura. Putnam, 1992. Europe in 1492: Scrupulous scholarship and outstanding visuals. (Grade 4 and up)

The Future-Telling Lady and Other Stories by James Berry. Perlman, 1993. Wealth of detail about life in the West Indies. (Grade 5 and up)

The Golden Deer retold by Margaret Hodges. Scribner's, 1992. A retelling of a Jataka tale provides a good entry into the traditional culture of India, Buddhism, and reincarnation. (Grades 2–4)

The Golden Guides; these books are extremely useful for middle-grade interest and research. Most libraries have them. Titles include *Birds*, *Insects*, *Fishes*, *Sea Shells*, and *Seashores of the World*. (Grades 3–6)

Gregory Cool by Caroline Binch. Dial, 1994. A visit to grandmother in Tobago produces a multicultural message. (Grades K–3)

Haiti in Pictures by the Department of Geography Staff. Visual Geography Series. Lerner, 1987. (Grade 5 and up)

Haiti Singing retold by Harold Courlander. Cooper, 1973. Reprint of 1939 edition by this now-deceased noted folklorist. (Grade 4 and up)

Haitian Americans by Nina Vehiller. People of North America Series. Chelsea, 1991. (Grade 5 and up)

How the Sea Began: A Taino Myth by George Crespo. Clarion, 1993. Puerto Rican Indian legend. Good to read aloud. (Grades 2–4)

How to Hunt Buried Treasure by James Deem. Houghton, 1992. The art of hunting many kinds of treasure. (Grade 4 and up)

How We Learned the Earth Is Round by Patricia Lauber. Let's Read-and-Find-Out Science Books. Crowell, 1990. Simple explanation. (Grades K–3)

Hue Boy by Rita Mitchell. Dial, 1993. Caribbean village life insights. (Grades K–2)

Insects by Althea. The Nature Club Series. Troll, 1990. (Grades 2–5)

Island Baby by Holly Keller. Greenwillow, 1992. An injured flamingo is nursed back to health in a setting beautifully reflecting the island landscape. (Grades K–3)

An Island Christmas by Lynn Joseph. Clarion, 1992. Trinidad and Tobago traditional Christmas celebration: picking red petals for the sorrel drink, mixing up the black currant cake, and singing along with the parang band. (Grades K–3)

Jamaica in Pictures by the Department of Geography Staff. Visual Geography Series. Lerner, 1987. (Grade 5 and up)

Jasmine's Parlour Day by Lynn Joseph. Lothrop, Lee & Shepard, 1994. Simple story of island life: Jasmine's Parlour is a food stand set up on a Trinidad beach. (Grades K–3)

Juan Bobo: Four Folktales from Puerto Rico retold by Carmen Bernier-Grand. HarperCollins, 1994. Tales from rural Puerto Rico. Spanish translation provided. (Grades K–3)

Kwanzaa by Deborah Chocolate. Children's, 1990. How African Americans celebrate their roots and cultural heritage. (Grades 3–5)

Kwanzaa by A. Porter. Carolrhoda, 1991. Origins and practices. (Grades 1–3)

The Land and People of Spain by Adrian Shubert. Portraits of the Nations Series. HarperCollins, 1992. History, geography, people, and culture. (Grade 4 and up)

Leroy the Lobster by Katherine Orr. Macmillan, 1985. The life story of the spiny lobster. (Grades K–2)

Lion & the Ostrich Chicks & Other African Tales retold by Ashley Bryan. Atheneum, 1986. Four stories representing various cultures of Africa define the black oral tradition. Bibliography. (Grades 4–6)

The Little Island by Frane Lessac. Dell, 1993. Montserrat is the setting of this story. (Grades 1–3)

The Log of Christopher Columbus: The First Voyage: Spring, Summer and Fall, 1492 selected by Steve Lowe from original sources. Philomel, 1992. (Grades 2–4)

The Magic Orange Tree and other Haitian Folktales collected by Diane Wolkstein. Schocken, 1987. Rare collection of folk tales and songs reflect the blend of cultures found in Haiti. (Grade 5 and up)

Misoso: Once-Upon-A-Time Tales from Africa retold by Verne Aardema. Knopf, 1994. Twelve folk tales from different parts of Africa. (Grades 3–5)

Moja Means One by Muriel Feelings. Dial, 1987. A Swahili counting book. (Grades K–3)

Morning Girl by Michael Dorres. Hyperion, 1992. A 12-year-old Taina girl and her younger brother witness the arrival of Columbus on a Bahamian island. A good picture of pre-Columbian life in the Caribbean. (Grades 4–6)

My Grandpa and the Sea by Katherine Orr. Carolrhoda, 1990. St. Lucia is the island setting. (Grades K–3)

My Name Is Not Angelica by Scott O'Dell. Houghton, 1989. Good to read aloud to class. Exciting historical fiction based on the St. John, Danish West Indies (now a U.S. Virgin Island), slave uprising. (Grade 5 and up)

My Two Worlds by Ginger Gordon. Clarion, 1993. Contrasts two worlds of an eight-year-old Dominican girl who lives in New York but frequently returns to her island home; exemplifies life in two interwoven cultures. (Grades K–3)

Night Reef: Dusk to Dawn on a Coral Reef by William Sargent. Watts, 1991. Beautiful underwater photos of coral-reef life in the Caribbean, Pacific, and Indian Oceans; accurate, clear, well-organized information. (Grade 5 and up)

The Oceans updated edition by Martyn Bramwell. Watts, 1994. Replaces 1987 edition. Includes glossary. (Grades 4–6)

Once Upon a Mouse adapted by Marcia Brown. Atheneum, 1961. Caldecott. A fable from the Indian Hitopadesa. (Grades K–4)

One Smiling Grandma: A Caribbean Counting Book by Ann Marie Linden. Dial, 1992. Sights a young girl sees on her island. (Grades K–2)

The Outside Dog by Charlotte Pomerantz. An "I Can Read Book." Harper, 1993. The setting for this book is Puerto Rico. Spanish words and phrases defined at the beginning of the book enhance the story. (Grades K–1)

The Ox of the Wonderful Horns and Other African Folk Tales by Ashley Bryan. Atheneum, 1993. Reissue of title first published in 1971. (Grades K–3)

Pedro's Journal: A Voyage With Christopher Columbus, August 3, 1492–February 14, 1493. Delacorte, 1992. Literary style lends immediacy to this fictional account. (Grades 3–5)

The People Who Hugged the Trees by Deborah Lee Rose. Holt, 1990. (Grades 4–8)

Perez y Martina, A Puerto Rican Folktale by Pura Belpre. Viking, 1991. Señorita Martina, a Spanish cockroach of high degree, marries a mouse. Reissue of a favorite traditional tale; excellent for reading aloud or storytelling. (Grades K–4)

Pirates by Daniel Defoe and Harry Knill. Bellerophon, 1975. Profusely illustrated, large format paperback. (Grades K–5)

Pirates of the Virgin Islands, The Golden Age of Piracy From 1690 to 1720 by Fritz Seyfarth and Barney Horntimber. Caribbean Adventure Books. Spanish Main, 1986. (Grade 4 and up)

Puerto Rico by Joyce Johnston. Hello U.S.A. Series. Lerner, 1994. (Grades 3–6)

Puerto Rico in Pictures by the Department of Geography Staff. Visual Geography Series. Lerner, 1987. (Grade 5 and up)

The Queen Conch by Katherine Orr. Windward, 1987. (Grades 3–5)

Rain Forest by Helen Cowcher. Soundpoints, 1989. Includes audiocassette. (Grades K–3)

Rain Forest Amerindians by Ana Lewington. Threatened Culture Series. Raintree Steck, 1992. (Grades 5–6)

Rain Forest Homes by Althea. Cambridge Natural History Series. Cambridge University, 1985. (Grade 1 and up)

Rata-Pata-Scata-Fata: A Caribbean Story by Phyllis Gershater. Little, Brown, 1994. Magic words to try to get the chores done. (Grades K–3)

Raw Head, Bloody Bones: African-American Tales of the Supernatural selected by Mary E. Lyons. Scribner's, 1991. Includes commentary on African folklore in the New World. (Grades 4–6)

The Renaissance by Tim Wood. Viking, 1993. Drawings, photos, and text describe fifteenth and sixteenth century European civilization during the discovery and exploration period of the New World. (Grade 4 and up)

Robinson Crusoe by Daniel DeFoe. Wyeth Illustrated Classics. Running Press, 1993. Read aloud to class but avoid abridgments. (Grade 4 and up)

The Search for the Right Whale by Scott Kraus. Crown, 1993. Follows a team of aquarium scientists as they follow and study a migrating endangered species. (Grade 4 and up)

Seashore by David Burnie. Eyewitness Explorers Series. Dorling Kindersley, 1994. Includes marine animals and plants, formation and changes, and so on. (Grade 4 and up)

Seashores by Joyce Pope. Nature Club Series. Troll, 1990. (Grades 3–6)

The Shell Book by Sandra Romaskko. Windward, 1984. Shells of the Atlantic Ocean, Gulf of Mexico, and Caribbean Sea. (Grades 2–5)

Shells by Jennifer Coldrey. Eyewitness Explorers Series. Dorling Kindersley, 1993. (Grade 3 and up)

Ship by David Macaulay. Houghton, 1993. Caribbean setting: A crew of archeologists salvages the remains of a 500-year-old caravel; then the story reverts to A.D. 1405 when the caravel was built. Outstanding illustrations. (Grade 4 and up)

Sing to the Sun by Ashley Bryan. HarperCollins, 1992. Poetry with a Caribbean beat: Short poems sing the praises of everyday joys. Riotous primary colors! (Grades K–6)

Slave Ship: The Story of the Henrietta Marie by George Sullivan. Cobblehill, 1994. A slave ship sinks 35 miles off the Florida coast in the early 1700s. (Grade 5 and up)

Snips & Snails & Walnut Whales by Phyllis Fiarotta. Workman, 1975. Nature crafts for children. (Grades 1–5)

Spiderman Anansi by James Berry. Holt, 1989. Twenty Anansi stories spring from Africa by way of the West Indies. (Grade 5 and up)

State Flags: Including the Commonwealth of Puerto Rico by Sue Brandt. Watts, 1992. History, design, and significance. (Grade 5 and up)

Stephen Biesty's Cross-Sections: Man-of-War by Stephen Biesty. Dorling Kindersley, 1993. Text and cutaway illustrations reveal a treasure of facts about life aboard a British warship of the Napoleonic era. (Grade 4 and up)

Story of the Dolphin by Katherine Orr. Carolrhoda, 1993. Respecting rights and feelings in a Caribbean setting. (Grades K–2)

The Tainos: The People Who Welcomed Columbus by Francine Jacobs. Putnam, 1992. "Momentous clash between two cultures." (Grade 4 and up)

Take a Trip to Haiti by John Griffiths. Watts, 1989. (Grades 3–5)

Take a Trip to Jamaica by Keith Lye. Watts, 1988. (Grades 3–5)

Tiger Soup: An Anansi Story from Jamaica retold by Frances Temple. Orchard, 1994. Good read-aloud; filled with easy rhythm of the Jamaican dialect. (Grades K–3)

Timothy of the Cay by Theodore Taylor. Harcourt, 1993. Sequel to *The Cay*. Boldly drawn novel about survival and race relations. (Grade 5 and up)

Tough Boris by Mem Fox. Harcourt, 1994. Boris Von der Borchis is a tough pirate, but he cries when his parrot dies. (Grades K–3)

Tracks in the Sand by Loreen Leedy. Doubleday, 1993. Eggs laid in sand hatch into tiny turtles that grow large enough to lay their own eggs. (Grades K–3)

Treasure Island by Robert Louis Stevenson. Wyeth Illustrated Classics. Running Press, 1993. A classic adventure to read aloud to class. There are many excellent, unabridged editions available. (Grade 5 and up)

Turtle Knows Your Name retold by Ashley Bryan. Atheneum, 1989. West Indian folk tale about a boy with a long name. (Grades 1–3)

Turtles by Cousteau Society Staff. Little Simon Series. Simon & Schuster, 1992. Physical characteristics, behavior, and life cycle of the sea turtle. (Grades K–2)

Undersea Homes by Althea. Cambridge Natural History Series. Cambridge University Press, 1986. (Grade 2 and up)

The Visual Dictionary of Ships and Sailing. Dorling Kindersley, 1991. The detailed cutaways are works of art. Nautical terminology includes all kinds of ships, signals, flags, and gear worn and used by sailors. (Grades K–6)

A Wave in Her Pocket by Lynn Joseph. Clarion, 1991. Six stories that combine Trinidad's traditional folklore with a child's view of island life. (Grade 4 and up)

Weather updated by Martyn Bramwell. Earth Science Library. Watts, 1994. Replaces 1987 edition; includes glossary. (Grades 4–6)

West Indian Folk Tales told by Sir Philip Sherlock. Oxford, 1966. Twenty-one tales of ancient people (Arawaks and Caribs) are interwoven with African slave folklore. (Grades 4–6)

Whales by John Wexo. Zoobooks, 1992. (Grades K–3)

What Is a Fish? by David Eastman. Now I Know Series. Troll, 1982. (Grades K–2)

What Lives in a Shell? by Kathleen Zoehfeld. Let's Read and Find Out Series. HarperCollins, 1994. Accurate information and illustrations. (Grades K–2)

Who Discovered America? Mysteries and Puzzles of the New World by Patricia Lauber. HarperCollins, 1992. Archeological discoveries reveal pre-Columbian exploration and early settlement data. (Grades 3–5)

Why the Sun and the Moon Live in the Sky retold by Elphinstone Dayrell. Houghton, 1968. Folk tale from eastern Nigeria, Africa. (Grades 2–3)

Windows on the Deep: The Adventures of an Underwater Explorer, Sylvia Earle by Andrea Conley. Watts, 1991. Career guidance for sea lovers. (Grade 4 and up)

Wonders of the Sea by Louis Sabin. Troll, 1982. (Grades 2–4)

The World in 1492 by Jean Fritz. Holt, 1992. Arranged continent by continent, except North and South America are combined. (Grade 5 and up)

Bibliography of Resources for Parents and Teachers

Caribbean Music

Calypso Folk Sing by Massie Paterson and Sammy Heyward. Ludlow Music, 1963.

Caribbean Carnival: Songs of the West Indies by Irving Burgie. Tambourine, 1992.

A Century of Progress in American Song by Marx and Anne Oberndorfer. Hall and McCreary, 1933.

Climbing Jacob's Ladder: Heroes of the Bible in African-American Spirituals edited by John Langstaff. McElderry, 1991. Companion volume to *What a Morning!*

Echoes of Africa in Folk Songs of the Americas by Beatrice Landeck. David McKay, 1961.

Exploring Music, Book 5 and Book 6 by Eunice Boardman and Beth Landis. Holt, 1966.

A Fiesta of Folk Songs from Spain and Latin America by Henrietta Yurchenco. Putnam, 1967.

Folk Songs of the Caribbean by Jim Morse. Bantam, 1958.

Jamaican Music by Michael Burnett. Oxford, 1982.

Jamaican Song and Story: Annancy Stories, Digging Sings, Dancing Tunes and Ring Tunes by Walter Jekyll. Dover, 1966.

Rain Forest Music by Jim Valley. Wright, 1991.

Sing, Children, Sing by Leonard Bernstein and Carl Miller. Chappell, 1972.

Songs of the Sailor and Lumberman by William H. Doerflinger. Meyerbooks, 1990.

The Trinidad Calypso: A Study of the Calypso in Oral Literature by Keith Warner. Heinemann, 1982.

Reggae for Kids: A Collection of Music for Kids of All Ages by Dr. and Mrs. Dread. RAS Records, 1992. Audiocassette.

Rounder Records. Smithsonian Folkways. Representative Caribbean music on vinyl records.

Steel Pan Favorites. CD recorded at Turtle Point Studio, St. Thomas, V.I. Gutu, 1991.

The West Indian Song Book for Group and Community Singing by Irving Burgie, Caribe Music Corp., 1972.

Windjammer by Louis de Rochemont. Original music score by Morton Gould. Columbia, 1970.

Your Caribbean Souvenir Songbook by Irving Burgie. Cherry Lane, 1990. Includes accompanying cassette.

*For brochure of Caribbean Music write: Parrot Fish Music, No. 2 Store Tvaer Gade, St. Thomas, V.I. 00802.

Caribbean Cookbooks

Caribbean Adventures: Classic Cajun Cooking and Tales From the Reign of the Pirates by Ed Landry. Adlai House, 1994.

Caribbean and African Cooking by Rosamund Grant. Interlink, 1993.

Caribbean Cooking by Davinia Sookia. Book Sales, 1994.

Caribbean Food and Drink by Aviva Paraiso. Bookwright Press, 1989.

Chili Pepper. Out West Publishing. Bi-monthly periodical with frequent articles on ethnic cuisines including in-depth articles on the Caribbean area.

Cooking Caribe by Christopher Idone and Helen McEachrane. Clarkson Potter, 1992.

Fruits and Vegetables of the Caribbean by M. J. Bourne et al. Macmillan Education, 1990. Not a cookbook but an excellent source about unfamiliar ingredients; clearly illustrated with color photographs.

Little Caribbean Cookbook by Jill Hamilton. Chronicle Books, 1990.

Maverick Sea Fare: A Caribbean Cook Book by Dee Carstarphen. Banyan, 1982.

Puerto Rican & Caribbean Cookbook edited by Raoul Gordon. Gordon Press, 1982.

A Taste of Cuba by Linette Creen. NAL-Dutton, 1994. Traditional recipes.

Traveling Jamaica With Knife, Fork & Spoon by Robb Welsh and Jay McCarthy. The Crossing, 1995.

Caribbean Crafts

Art From Many Hands by Jo Miles Schuman. Davis, 1981.

Box Art by Don Mellack. Crown Arts and Crafts, 1975.

Caribbean Festival Arts: Each and Every Bit of Difference by John Nunley and Judith Bettleheim. The St. Louis Art Museum in association with University of Washington Press, 1988. Published on the occasion of the exhibition Caribbean Festival Arts by the St. Louis Art Museum, December 1988.

The Costume Book for Parties and Plays by Joseph Leeming. Lippincott, 1966. Classic source for costume construction.

Easy to Make Columbus Discovers America Diorama by A. G. Smith. Dover, 1990.

Introducing Batik by Evelyn Samuel. William Clowes, 1983.

Kites That Fly: A Classic by Leslie Hunt. **Twenty-five Kites That Fly** by Leslie Hunt. Dover 1971. Reprint of 1929 classic.

Little Tropical Fish Coloring Book by Ellen McHenry. Dover, 1994.

Macramé: The Art of Creative Knotting by Virginia Harvey. Van Nostrand Reinhold, 1987.

My First Nature Book by Angela Walker. Knopf, 1990.

Nature With Children of All Ages by Edith Sisson. Prentice Hall, 1987.

Of Hands and Earth (Virgin Islands Crafts Using Natural Resources) by Dana Ulsamer-Harrison. 1992.

The Remarkable Rainforest by Toni Albert. Trickle Creek Books, 1994. "An active-learning book for kids."

Tropical Flowers of the World Coloring Book by Lynda Chandler. Pictorial Archives Services. Dover, 1981.

Other Media

Tears of Haiti, University of Pittsburgh, 1988. Documentary film.

Dominican Republic, Cradle of The Americas, Museum of Modern Art of Latin America, Washington, D.C. Videocassette in English; 25 minutes in length.

Posters

The World Harvest includes chilis, gourds, beans, potatoes, maize, and tomatoes. Florida Museum of Natural History, University of Florida.

Teacher Materials

Against Borders: Promoting Books for a Multi-Cultural World by Hazel Rochman. American Library Association, 1993. Subject access by ethnic group and nationality; useful for developing units on ethnic and cultural diversity.

Ancient Forests: Discovering Nature by Margaret Anderson et al. Dog-Eared, 1994.

Animals of the Tropical Rain Forest by Judy Ling. Sunshine Reading Series, 1994.

The Baedeker's Caribbean. Prentice Hall, 1992.

The Bahamas. Fodor, 1993.

Beachcombers Field Guide to Shells by Idaz Greenberg. Seahawk, 1985. Includes plastic card with shells listed and pictured for easy reference or enlargement for display. Others in series include *Field Guide to Marine Invertebrates*, and *Game Fishes of the Tropical Atlantic*.

A Brief History of the Caribbean by Jan Rogozinski. Facts on File, 1992. From the Arawak and the Carib to the present.

The Caribbean: Essence of the Islands by Bill Smith. Little, Brown, 1989. Information on Carnival in Martinique.

The Caribbean Islands by Hans Hannau. Doubleday, 1972. Full-color photographs.

Caribbean Islands Handbook edited by Ben Box and Sarah Cameron. Trade and Travel, 1992.

The Folklore of World Holidays edited by Margaret Read. Gale, 1992. Excludes the United States.

Herbs and Proverbs of the Virgin Islands by Arona Peterson. St. Joseph's Graphics, St. Thomas, V.I., 1974.

Inside Biosphere 2: The Rainforest by Karen Liptale. Biosphere Press, 1994.

Insight Guides Series. Houghton. Includes the following titles: *Barbados*, 1993; *Cuba*, 1995; *Jamaica*, 1995; *Puerto Rico*, 1995; and *Trinidad & Tobago*, 1993.

Islands of Beauty and Bounty translated by Nina York. St. Croix, 1986. Historical profile of the Danish West Indies, including an excellent description of the sugar-cane industry when it was flourishing on St. Croix.

Isles of the Caribbean by Tor Eigelund et al. National Geographic, 1980.

Isles of the Caribbees by Carlton Mitchell. National Geographic, 1966. A classic if available.

Jamaica Handbook by Karl Luntta. Moon, 1993.

Kaleidoscope: A Multi-Cultural Booklist for Grades K–8 by Rudine Bishop, editor, and NCTE Multicultural Booklist Committee. NCTE, 1994. Includes Caribbean.

Look Inside a Rainforest translated by Alexandra Fischer. Grosset & Dunlap, 1994.

M Caribbean Series includes the following titles: *Caribbean Carnivals & Festivals, Caribbean A–Z, Historic Caribbean,* and *Caribbean Sights and Sounds.* Also includes a series of natural history booklets on local subjects with outstanding photographs. Macmillan Education.

O Brave New Words! Native American Loanwords in Current English by Charles L. Cutler. University of Oklahoma Press, 1994.

Ole Time Sayin's: Proverbs of the West Indies by Lito Valls. 1983.

101 Questions and Answers—Cars, Planes, Ships and Trains by Ian Graham. Facts on File, 1995.

Qué Pasa. Box 4435, Old San Juan Station, San Juan, Puerto Rico 00905. Quarterly tourist magazine; emphasizes the past and present culture of Puerto Rico. Will respond to inquiries.

See Inside a Galleon by Jonathan Rutland. Warick, 1978.

Seeds of Change: A Quincentennial Celebration edited by Herman Viola and Carolyn Margolis. Smithsonian Institution Press, 1991.

Still a Nation of Immigrants by Brent Ashabranner. Cobblehill, 1993. Identifies today's immigrants; includes how an immigrant becomes a citizen.

Venture Into Cultures: A Resource Book of Multicultural Materials and Programs. The American Library Association, 1992. Indexed by culture, including African, American, Arabic, Hispanic, Jewish, and Persian. (Grades K–8)

The World on the Move: Water Travel by Eryl Davies. Thompson, 1993.

Index